PUTTING ON THE ARMOR

EQUIPPED AND DEPLOYED FOR SPIRITUAL WARFARE

CHUCK LAWLESS

Published by LifeWay Press®
Nashville, Tennessee

ISBN 1-4158-3204-8

This book is a resource in the Bible Studies category of the
Christian Growth Study Plan.
Course CG-1198

Dewey Decimal Classification: 235.4
Subject Headings: SPIRITUAL WARFARE \ SPIRITUAL LIFE

Unless otherwise noted, all Scripture quotations are taken from the Holman Christian
Standard Bible®, copyright © 1999, 2000, 2001, 2002, 2003 by Holman Bible Publishers.
Used by permission.

Scripture quotations marked NASB are taken from the New American Standard Bible®,
Copyright © 1960, 1962, 1963, 1968, 1971, 1972, 1973, 1975, 1977, 1995 by
The Lockman Foundation. Used by permission. (*www.lockman.org*)

Scripture quotations marked NIV are taken from the Holy Bible, New International Version,
Copyright © 1973, 1978, 1984 by International Bible Society.

Scripture quotations marked KJV are from the King James Version of the Bible.

Scripture quotations marked RSV are from the Revised Standard Version of the Bible,
copyright 1946, 1952, © 1971, 1973 by the National Council of the
Churches of Christ in the U.S.A., and used by permission.

To order additional copies of this resource:
WRITE LifeWay Church Resources Customer Service;
One LifeWay Plaza; Nashville, TN 37234-0113; FAX order to (615) 251-5933;
PHONE (800) 458-2772; ORDER ONLINE at *www.lifeway.com*;
E-MAIL *orderentry@lifeway.com*; or VISIT the LifeWay Christian Store serving you.

Printed in the United States of America

Leadership and Adult Publishing
LifeWay Church Resources
One LifeWay Plaza
Nashville, TN 37234-0175

TABLE OF CONTENTS

MEET THE AUTHOR

CHUCK LAWLESS is the dean of the Billy Graham School of Missions, Evangelism, and Church Growth at The Southern Baptist Theological Seminary in Louisville, KY. For the past 10 years he served as senior associate dean under the leadership of Dr. Thom Rainer, now president of LifeWay Christian Resources.

He has said his goal as dean is "to produce what I call 'discipled warriors,' who march into battle wearing the full armor of God." His mission is to be a Great Commission school with Acts 1:8 impact.

Dr. Lawless is a two-time graduate of Southern Seminary, having completed both a master of divinity and doctor of philosophy degree in evangelism and church growth. A native of Mason, Ohio, he is a popular speaker and preacher.

In 2002 he received the Findley B. and Louvenia Edge Award for Teaching Excellence at Southern Seminary, an honor conferred by a vote of the student body and faculty.

A prolific writer, Dr. Lawless has written six books, including *Discipled Warriors: Growing Healthy Churches That Are Equipped for Spiritual Warfare*. His wife Pam is his "prayer warrior" as he fulfills God's calling to the subject of spiritual warfare.

Dr. Lawless cowrote the popular LifeWay resource *Spiritual Warfare: Biblical Truth for Victory*. Lawless describes *Putting on the Armor* as an enhanced version of chapter 6 of the original book and the next step for those who have completed that study. While this second study stands alone, both are needed for the practical insights that will benefit not only the individual but also the family and church.

DIANE NOBLE contributed the worksheets and leader guide for *Putting on the Armor*. She is the former director of discipleship and women's ministries at First Baptist Church, Harrisonville, Missouri, where her husband David serves as pastor. Diane has an extensive background in curriculum design and development. She earned a bachelor of arts degree in education from William Jewell College in Liberty, Missouri, and a master of arts degree in education administration from Truman State University in Kirksville, Missouri. The Nobles have two grown sons.

INTRODUCTION

I hope you have chosen to do this study because you are interested in the topic of spiritual warfare. If so, you're not alone. Since the late 1980s, hundreds of books about the topic have been published. Many Web sites address the topic. Perhaps you've even completed the previous study that John Franklin and I cowrote—*Spiritual Warfare: Biblical Truth for Victory* (Lifeway, 2001). Wherever your interest lies, I'm glad that you're joining me for these seven weeks. Although I may not know you by name, I'm praying for you as you begin. My prayer is that God will deploy you into your community with the gospel, fully armed and equipped for the battle.

This resource is designed primarily for group use, although individuals will benefit from personal study as well. It focuses on the armor of God passage in Ephesians 6:10-20. For six weeks, you will study a different piece of the armor. Each day's lesson will include activities to reinforce what you learn from God's Word. On the first day of each new week, you will have opportunity to review all of the armor pieces previously studied. Week 7 emphasizes "The Power of Prayer" that closes Paul's section on the armor pieces.

Week 1 teaches the basics of spiritual warfare and will help you become familiar with the outline of the overall study. Beginning with day 2 of week 1, I'll challenge you to read through the Book of Ephesians in the optional "Daily in the Word" assignment at the end of each lesson.

I want to help you to read this book systematically because I believe so strongly that the Word of God is a powerful weapon against the Enemy. You will also find a suggested verse to memorize each week. Hiding God's Word in your heart will equip you with ready inspiration and ammunition when the Devil pursues you.

The activities in your five-day-a-week study should be completed on your own during the week. The activities will help you apply to your life what you learn. In the margins of the lessons you will find additional information such as word studies and Bible passages.

Spiritual warfare does not need to be a mysterious unseen process; the basis for victory in spiritual warfare is a personal love relationship with Jesus Christ. If you have not yet acknowledged Him as Lord of your life, turn to page 147 and read "The ABCs of Salvation."

Let me pray for you as you begin this study.

Father, I thank You for Your Word that shows us how to win spiritual battles, and I'm grateful for each person who has chosen to do this study. I pray that each one will see You more than they see the Enemy, love You more than anything the Enemy offers, and experience victory (God's will for you) more than defeat. God, I ask You to equip all of us in Your armor and then deploy us as Your witnesses throughout the world. Thank You that we can march forward in victory, empowered by Your Holy Spirit.

In Jesus' name I pray,

Chuck Lawless

The Belt of Truth

Ed and Ann Miller, a Christian couple, have worked diligently to rear their three children. Jason, the oldest, has just returned home on break after his third year in college. Al, the second son, just turned 19, and daughter Reba is 16. Around the family dinner table one night, Jason surprised his parents with these questions: "How do we know that Christianity is true? And what makes us believe that theories like evolution aren't true?"

Immediately, Jason's parents assumed that his college professors had filled their son's head with lies from the Enemy. They began to pray against the influence of the professors, asking God to protect Jason from their false teachings. They didn't want the father of lies to win the battle in their son's life. Meanwhile, Jason wondered if there are universal truths—absolutes, regardless of the situation—and how you know if they are true.

In week 1 we will explore the issue of truth. Truth is a person, Jesus Christ; a written body of Scripture, the Bible; and what we feel, say, and do in everyday life. Knowing the truth equips us for discerning the presence and purposes of Satan in our lives.

day  *one*

PREPARATION FOR THE BATTLE

"Put on the full armor of God so that you can stand against the tactics of the Devil. For our battle is not against flesh and blood, but against the rulers, against the authorities, against the world powers of this darkness, against the spiritual forces of evil in the heavens."
Ephesians 6:11-12

The background of this study is the Book of Ephesians, a letter that the Apostle Paul wrote to believers around the area of Ephesus in Asia Minor. This letter neatly divides into two major sections: the theological foundation (chapters 1–3) and the practical application (chapters 4–6). In the second section, Paul warned that we are in a spiritual war and must put on the full armor of God in order to win this battle.

Read Ephesians 6:11-12 in the margin.

In this text Paul clearly indicated who our enemy is not and who our enemy is. We don't wrestle against human beings ("flesh and blood"), even though we may

wrongly assume that other people are the problem. Paul wrote this letter from a prison cell, where it would have been easy for him to see the guards who held him as the enemy. Instead, he saw them as people God loved and who needed salvation (see Acts 16:22-34). How different our churches would be if we remembered Paul's teaching that our war isn't against one another!

How would you counsel Ed and Ann Miller? For example, were the college professors the real problem?

_____

_____

Christians battle against a supernatural enemy ("the Devil"), whose forces would overwhelm us except for the presence of God in our lives. In fact, Paul used multiple terms (*rulers, authorities, world powers,* and *spiritual forces*) to describe the innumerable powers that stand against us.

Paul was not the only Bible writer to describe this battle. Match each scriptural passage with its corresponding story.

_____ 1. Genesis 3:15   A. Satan enticed David to take a census.

_____ 2. 1 Chronicles 21:1   B. The Devil will ultimately be bound.

_____ 3. Job 1:1-22   C. Satan caused chaos in the life of a righteous man.

_____ 4. 1 Peter 5:8   D. The snake (Satan) will be defeated by someone from the seed of the woman (Christ, from the seed of Mary).

_____ 5. Revelation 20:1-3   E. The Enemy seeks to devour believers.

A tactician who entices us to sin, this very real Enemy causes disorder in our lives and seeks to devour us. Just listen to some of his names, and you'll get a sense of his character: accuser, adversary, the Devil, the dragon, the Evil One, the god of this age, the father of lies, the serpent, the tempter. This Enemy is not one with whom we want to tangle in our own power.

Good news, however, prevails: God planned from the beginning to defeat the Enemy and did so through the death of Jesus (Gen. 3:15; Col. 2:15). Now we can live in victory by putting on the full armor of God. As we will see, putting on the armor requires believing and acting according to God's Word. When we do both, we are equipped and deployed for spiritual warfare.

What We Believe Is Important in Spiritual Warfare

To see the truth of this statement, read the story of Ananias and Sapphira (Acts 5:1-11).

What beliefs do you think led Ananias and Sapphira to act deceitfully?

_____

_____

Now read about Peter and John in Acts 4:13-22. What beliefs do you think led them to act obediently?

_____

_____

Perhaps Ananias and Sapphira believed their additional wealth was more important than truthfulness and holiness. Maybe they believed they would have opportunity to make the situation right later on. They likely believed that they could hide their sin or that God wouldn't judge them for their secret. Whatever the case, Ananias and Sapphira ultimately acted based on incorrect beliefs.

On the other hand, Peter and John believed that obedience to the Father was more important than anything the Enemy threatened. They chose to risk their lives on the truth of Jesus' death and resurrection. Right beliefs led them to right actions. Paul, too, understood this truth. In the first three chapters of Ephesians he laid the theological foundation (that is, the beliefs) for our victory in spiritual warfare.

You will want to open your Bible to Ephesians and read each of these referenced verses showing us that believers are in Christ.

We are chosen in Him (Eph. 1:4) and have "redemption through His blood" (1:7). In Him we have an inheritance (1:11). Our hope is in Him (1:12), and He has sealed us (1:13). Through Him we now have "boldness, access, and confidence through faith" (3:12). If we believe these truths—that Christ has chosen us, sealed us, and given us access to the Father—we should also believe that *in Christ* we can win spiritual battles. Right beliefs are essential for engaging the Enemy.

How I wish somebody had taught me about my identity in Christ when I was a young believer! I knew that God had saved me, but I lived a defeated Christian life for several years while I tried in my own strength to be obedient to God. No one showed me the importance of who I am in Christ. Now, I know that right beliefs would have helped me fight the battles I faced.

Right beliefs are essential for engaging the Enemy.

Check (✔) the statements that most reflect your current viewpoint.

_____ 1. I'm grateful for who I am in Christ.
_____ 2. I haven't thought much about my position in Christ.
_____ 3. I'm not certain that I am in Christ.
_____ 4. I want to learn more about who I am in Christ.
_____ 5. I know who I am in Christ and have been experiencing
        daily spiritual victories.
_____ 6. My actions don't generally show that I am in Christ.
_____ 7. I'm growing in Christ, but I still struggle with obedience.

More In-Depth Study
In the first three chapters of Ephesians, highlight the phrases "in Christ,"
"in Christ Jesus," "in Him," "through Jesus Christ," "through Him," "of Him,"
and "with the Messiah." Then meditate on all of the blessings Paul wrote
that we receive because we are "in Him." Thank God for these blessings.

What We Do Is Also Important in Spiritual Warfare

While right beliefs are important, they alone aren't always enough to defeat
the Enemy. In fact, even the demons rightly believe in one God and shudder
(Jas. 2:19)—but their actions are evil. Right beliefs must lead to right actions,
and those right actions defeat the Enemy.

In the last three chapters of Ephesians, Paul described a life characterized by
church unity (Eph. 4:1-16), personal holiness (4:17–5:21), and Christlike relationships in our homes (5:22–6:4) and in our workplaces (6:5-9). Paul essentially said
that what we believe must affect every area of our lives. How can we say we believe
something if those beliefs don't change the way we live?

Look back at those areas that Paul described in Ephesians 4–6: personal holiness, godly relationships in our home, Christian living before our coworkers, and
unity in the church. Achieving any of these goals is never easy because the Enemy
strikes against us and our relationships. He delights when our lifestyle reflects
him more than God. He loves it when our homes are fractured and workplaces
disturbed by bad attitudes and poor choices. The Devil is especially pleased when
church members see other believers as the enemy and attack one another. God's
plan is for unity among believers (see John 17:22-23). When arguing and fighting
occur in a church, our witness to the world is seriously weakened.

> Right beliefs must lead to right actions, and those right actions defeat the Enemy.

**Mark any of these areas where the Enemy currently seems to be
attacking you.**

❑ My personal holiness—I am struggling with sin issues.
❑ My workplace—I am not getting along with someone there.
❑ My family—our relationships are strained.
❑ My church—some division is occurring in the congregation.

The way to counter the Enemy's arrows is to live obediently in Christ—and that's
why what we do matters in spiritual warfare. We will discover in this study that
putting on the whole armor of God is all about obedience. Only obedient warriors
are equipped to be deployed in the spiritual battle.

> The whole armor of God is all about obedience.

9

Getting Started

As we study together, keep in mind these seven truths about the armor of God:

1. We are to wear the full armor of God. We will study each piece separately, but don't forget that we must wear *all* of the armor.

2. The armor we wear is God's armor (Eph. 6:11). We would never win these battles if we were to use our own armor.

3. Putting on the armor is nothing magical. Wearing the armor is more about personal spiritual disciplines than "praying on" the equipment each day.

4. Wearing the armor can't be separated from what we believe and how we live. Our belief system (theology) influences our behavior. Both are important and work together as we face spiritual battles.

5. Putting on the armor is about being equipped and deployed for spiritual battles. Wearing the armor isn't just preparation for the battle; it's also part of the battle as the Enemy fights to keep us from wearing the armor.

6. The support of other believers helps us put on the armor. Paul wrote his letter to "the saints and believers" (Eph. 1:1), and he expected them to stand together in the battle. If you're completing this study alone, enlist a group of prayer warriors to support you as you study. If you are meeting with a group, their encouragement will prove invaluable.

7. Learning about the armor of God takes place only as we read God's Word. As you will learn throughout this study, the Word of God teaches us about each piece of the armor. That's also why, beginning with tomorrow's study, I'll encourage you to read a portion of the Book of Ephesians each day.

To review these important truths, read each one again and fill in the blanks. Remember these major points.

1. We are to wear the _____ armor of God.

2. The armor we wear is _____ armor.

3. Putting on the armor is nothing _____.

4. Wearing the armor can't be separated from what we _____

   and how we _____.

5. Putting on the armor is about being _____ and _____

   for spiritual battles.

6. The support of other _____ helps us put on the armor.

7. Learning about the armor of God takes place only as we read

   God's _____.

Answers to activity on page 7: 1. D; 2. A; 3. C; 4. E; 5. B

day  *two*

FINDING TRUTH IN THE WORD OF GOD

Maybe your story mirrors Kaleisha's. Unchurched for most of her life, she became a Christian when a teenage friend told her about Christ. During her second week in church, she heard her pastor challenge the church to read the Word daily. He spoke so strongly and so passionately that she knew this commitment must be important. She assumed that "the Word of God" meant the Bible, so Kaleisha decided to read it daily. Embarrassed by her lack of knowledge, she feared asking anyone for help in getting started.

The next morning, she awakened early and grabbed the Bible her friend had given her. Her questions quickly mounted. Where should I begin? What's a "testament"? What's the difference between the Old Testament and the New Testament? Why are there different books and chapters in the Bible? What do I do with the words I don't understand or can't pronounce? Overwhelmed by this foreign book, Kaleisha laid it aside that morning. This pattern continued for several months until an older believer began to mentor her. Only then did she start to understand the importance of knowing the truths of the Word of God.

Days 3-5 focus on wearing *the belt of truth* as one piece of our spiritual armor. Reading and knowing God's Word—the Bible—equips us to wear this belt. Week 6 focuses much more on the Bible (the "sword of the Spirit"), but week 1 is critical to understanding what is true and how to wear this first piece of God's armor.

The Word of God Is Truth

Satan is a liar, and the truth isn't in him (John 8:44). He established his pattern in the garden of Eden when he lied to Adam and Eve about the truthfulness of God's Word (Gen. 3:1-5). That pattern has not changed. To this day, the Enemy wants us to doubt or ignore God's Word; after all, if it's not *God's* Word in the first place, why should we read and follow it?

Let's look at one believer for whom the truth of the Word was life-changing. Timothy was a young man who caught the attention of the Apostle Paul as he traveled through the cities of Derbe and Lystra (Acts 16:1-3). Others spoke well of Timothy, and Paul wanted him as a student and partner in ministry. For the next several years, Paul mentored young Timothy and eventually challenged him to "fulfill his ministry" even as Paul faced his own death (2 Tim. 4:1-8).

What we know about Timothy's upbringing is sketchy, but we do know that his mother and grandmother taught him the sacred writings of Scripture (2 Tim. 1:5; 3:14-17). Those writings changed Timothy's life and equipped him to battle the Enemy. Such is the power and truth of God's Word. Has anyone ever challenged you to memorize Scripture? Maybe you're not accustomed to learning Sunday School verses or searching the Word during Bible drills. Learning Scriptures is not just for children! It's not too late for you to begin this habit.

Read Psalm 19:7-11 and write the words that describe the Bible.

_____

David the psalmist fully understood that the Word is perfect, trustworthy, right, radiant, pure, reliable, and rewarding. That Word, he said, revives the soul, makes the inexperienced wise, makes the heart glad, enlightens the eyes, and warns God's servants. Living according to Scripture's truths enables us to keep our way pure.

The Devil's lies are simply no match for the Word of God. Jesus used the perfect, true Word of God to defeat Satan at the mount of temptation (Matt. 4:1-11). Because God's Word is truth, we must read it to wear the belt of truth. We would not know the truth of Jesus—who *is* the Word (John 1:1)—apart from the authors who were inspired to write the Word. Nor would we know about the reality of the Enemy we face. The Word not only warns us of the battle but shows us how to experience victory in Christ.

What is your commitment to Bible reading? Place an "x" on the spot that best indicates your current practice.

1	2	3	4	5
I am not reading at all.	I read occasionally.	I read about once a month.	I read at least once a week.	I read daily.

We Must Read, Interpret, and Apply This Truth

In week 6 we will look at different methods of Bible study. For now, let's look at some basic principles for reading and understanding the Word. Remember, we must know the truth—God's Word—to stand against an Enemy who lies.

Study the Word systematically. God inspired the entire Bible, and He expects us to read it in its entirety. How we do so may vary, but we should have a plan that guides us through the Scriptures. I will give you some suggested plans when we look at the sword of the Spirit in week 6.

Learn to interpret the Word properly. Reading the Bible is only one step in using God's Word to defeat the Enemy. We must also understand the Word properly before applying its teachings in our lives. These basic guidelines will help you interpret the meaning of Bible chapters and verses.

1. Read the text in more than one translation, noting the differences.
2. Understand the type of writing you are reading (for example: a Gospel, an Epistle, one of the Prophets, a history, and so forth).
3. Using appropriate Bible study tools, examine the cultural and historical background of the passage. Most study Bibles have this information.
4. Read the passage in its context in the specific book of the Bible and how that book fits in to the Bible as a whole. For example, is it in the Old Testament or New Testament? Do both testaments contain these thoughts?

Key Definitions

Testament—meaning "covenant"; one of two major divisions in the Bible

Gospel—one of the first four books of the New Testament that tells the "good news" of Jesus' life

Epistle—one of the letters in the New Testament written to a person, church, or group of believers

Prophets—spokesmen such as Isaiah who challenged God's people to live according to His standards

Hermeneutics—the process of interpreting verses from the Bible

5. Always look for the author's intended meaning in the passage. Every author chose words and expressions to convey a particular meaning. Good hermeneutics helps us to determine that meaning.

6. When necessary, allow more clearly and more frequently stated teachings to inform confusing passages.

7. To help you understand the text, don't hesitate to use commentaries, Sunday School or small-group materials, and other resources such as a Bible dictionary. That's what I've done as God led me to seek clarification on Ephesians 6:11-20.

Apply and live the Word daily. Reading and interpreting the Word properly are still not enough if we don't let the Word change our lives. Wearing the belt of truth means knowing Jesus personally, reading and understanding God's Word, and daily living out the Word's teachings. Learning to apply the Word will be the focus of day 4.

How well do you know how to read, interpret, and apply God's Word? Mark each statement true (*T*) or false (*F*).

_____ No one has ever taught me how to interpret the Bible.
_____ I feel confident that I know how to interpret the Bible properly.
_____ It's usually clear to me how Bible teachings apply to me.
_____ I often don't apply the Bible's teachings to my life.
_____ The Bible confuses me.
_____ I really haven't tried very hard to interpret the Bible.
_____ If I don't understand a passage, I have resources to help me.

More In-Depth Study
1. Read Isaiah 61:1-2. Use the seven guidelines listed to interpret this passage on your own paper.
2. Read Luke 4:16-21. Use the same guidelines to interpret it.
3. Compare the two passages.
4. Read Luke 4:22-30. How did the people in the synagogue feel about Jesus' interpretation of Isaiah 61:1-2?

"Daily in the Word" Will Help You Understand the Truth

Although this Bible study covering the entire Book of Ephesians is optional, consider this an invitation to join me in reading Ephesians during this study. Each day you'll read one portion of Ephesians, and I'll provide hints to help you interpret and apply it.

In your member book, highlight any truths that are especially meaningful to you. You may prefer underlining them or placing a star or asterisk by them. You may divide your reading between morning and night or read it in one sitting. Each week I'll also challenge you to memorize a verse from that week's readings. Memorize phrase by phrase until you can say the verse.

By the end of this study, you'll know Ephesians well. Today's study begins by providing background information about the book. Keep in mind that this information is important in understanding Paul's letter to Ephesus. Only when we understand and apply God's Word properly can we wear the belt of truth.

RESOURCES FOR BIBLE STUDY
- *Holman Illustrated Bible Dictionary*
- *Holman Bible Handbook*
- *Holman Old Testament and New Testament Commentary*
- *Resources by B & H Publishers and LifeWay Press*

Key Definitions

Heresy—departure from accepted belief or doctrine

Theology—the study of God and His teachings

Daily in the Word

AUTHOR: Paul wrote the book of Ephesians (see 1:1). Paul used Ephesus as a center for evangelism for three years (Acts 19–20).

DATE OF WRITING: Many date the letter around 60 A.D. If so, Paul would have written the letter during his Rome imprisonment.

TYPE OF LITERATURE: Ephesians is an epistle (a letter), likely written not only to the believers in Ephesus but also to other believers in the same region. This type of letter, known as a circular letter, went to Ephesus, an important commercial center in the region of Asia Minor (now Turkey). The Temple of Artemis (Diana), one of the seven wonders of the ancient world, was most prominent in Ephesus.

PURPOSE: Unlike other letters that Paul wrote, Ephesians does not address a particular problem or heresy in the church. Paul may have written the letter simply to strengthen and encourage the believers to be faithful, especially as they battled against the powers of darkness believed to be so prominent in the area of Ephesus. Paul wanted them to understand their position in Christ and their responsibility to be faithful to Him. For that reason, he addressed both theology and practical living.

SIMPLE OUTLINE:
1. Greeting (1:1-2)
2. The Believer's Position in Christ (1:3–3:21)
3. The Believer's Practice in Christ (4:1–6:9)
4. The Believer's Armor (6:10-20)
5. Final Greetings (6:21-23)

day three

WHO TRUTH IS

The week before Easter the Sunday School class seemed to be going well. The teacher talked passionately about Jesus, the Son of God, dying for the sins of the world. "Wait a minute," interrupted Jordan, a talkative guest in the class. "Jesus wasn't the Son of God. He was just a teacher who died because He made the religious leaders mad." Class members sat quietly, stunned by a statement they had seldom heard in church.

How would you have responded to Jordan? Be prepared to express your ideas in your next group session.

Even though Jordan was visiting a Sunday School class, he believed a lie. The Enemy is behind false teachings about Jesus Christ. Think about some of the other lies about Jesus you may have heard (and perhaps even believed at some point):
- Jesus is only one way of many routes to God.
- Jesus couldn't possibly have been born by a virgin.
- Jesus must have committed some sin during His lifetime.
- Jesus was a great prophet, but He was no more than that.
- Jesus died as a martyr, but He didn't die for the sins of the world.
- Jesus' bodily resurrection was only a myth circulated by the disciples.

The Enemy knows that if he can deceive us about Jesus and His work, he misleads us about the very cornerstone of the Christian faith. Apart from the crucifixion, burial, and resurrection of the perfect Son of God, we have no hope; so the Enemy aims his arrows at our understanding of Jesus. We must know Jesus—who is truth—in order to wear the belt of truth. Be certain that you understand who Jesus is and that you know Him personally.

Jesus Is the Truth

When Jesus told His disciples that He was going to prepare a place for them, Thomas questioned Him, "Lord … we don't know where You're going. How can we know the way?" Jesus' response was quick and clear: "I am the way, the truth, and the life" (see John 14:1-6).

What did Jesus mean when He said, "I am the truth"? One helpful writer put it this way: "Jesus is the very embodiment of truth. He is the truth in person."[1] His words, His actions, and His thoughts are always right. In Him there is no falsehood or deceit. As the one who is truth and life, He is the only way to the Father (John 14:6).

Several times, Jesus referred to the religious leaders of His day as "hypocrites" (see Matt. 6:2,5,16; 15:1-9; 23:1-39). These leaders looked good to an outsider: they gave to the poor, prayed in the synagogues, fasted according to their custom, tithed their incomes, and followed traditions of ritual cleansing. Unfortunately for them, however, Jesus knew what they were on the inside. They honored God with their lips, but their hearts were far from Him. They looked good—but only like a freshly-painted tombstone that in reality covered a dead body. In the end, they couldn't fool the One who is Truth.

The word *hypocrite* meant "actor," or one who is playing a role. As you think about wearing the belt of truth, are you seeking to follow Christ with absolute integrity, or are you guilty of "play acting" in your Christianity? Dave, a member of a church I pastored, "acted" his faith until the inner anguish of his hypocrisy cost him his peace and his health. "I can't do it anymore," he told me. "I can't fool the One who matters, so why do I try to fool others?" We could all benefit from asking that question of ourselves.

Jesus Knew the Truth

You've probably been in a situation when two people gave you completely different accounts of the same story. He says this, and she says that—and you are caught in the middle, trying to determine where the truth really lies. Never did Jesus find Himself in such a situation, for He who is truth *always* knew the truth.

"I am the way, the truth, and the life."—Jesus Christ
John 14:6

Read the following Bible texts from the Gospel of John. Write a brief description of what Jesus knew in each situation.

1. John 4:7-19 _____

_____

2. John 6:14-15 _____

_____

3. John 6:60-64 _____

_____

Jesus knew, and still knows, the truth in all situations. He knew past sins (John 4:7-19), current thoughts (6:14-15), and future actions (6:64). The Enemy lures us into sin, and he then wants us to hide our sin just as Adam and Eve attempted to do in the garden (Gen. 3:8). We somehow become convinced that hidden sin is acceptable sin. But no thought we think, no word we speak, and no action we take is hidden from the One who knows all truth.

Take a few minutes now to confess to Him, who knows all things, any hidden sin in your life. If you feel comfortable doing so, find another Christian who might hold you accountable in this area. I'll cover the concept of an accountability partner in day 5.

Jesus Spoke the Truth

The Old Testament was clear about the means to evaluate the validity of a prophet's words: if they did not come true, the prophet was no prophet after all (Deut. 18:21-22). Death was the penalty for being a false prophet (Deut. 18:20).

Apply that same standard to Jesus, and we learn that Jesus not only knew all truth, but He spoke it as well. He told the fishermen He would make them fishers of men (Matt. 4:19) and they would later become leaders in the early church.

Jesus promised His disciples that they would have authority over demons and disease, and they used that authority as they preached the gospel (Luke 9:1-6). He challenged a grieving father to believe that his daughter would live again, and the girl later "got up and began to walk" (see Mark 5:35-43). He also predicted His disciples' betrayals (Luke 22:31-34; John 13:21), warned of Jerusalem's destruction (Matt. 24:1-2), spoke of His impending death (John 12:27-33), and foretold His own resurrection (Matt. 20:17-19).

Jesus *is* the truth who *knows* the truth and *speaks* the truth. Indeed, He is the true Word of God (John 1:1). His Word promises He will forgive us (1 John 1:9), never leave us (Heb. 13:5), and return for us someday (1 Thess. 4:13-18), and we can trust those truths!

Read the words of Jesus in Revelation 22:12-13,20. Check (✔) each statement that describes your reaction to these verses.

"In the beginning was the Word, and the Word was with God, and the Word was God." John 1:1

1. ____ I know Jesus speaks truth when I read His Word or pray.
2. ____ I'm not certain that I believe Jesus' words.
3. ____ I know Jesus speaks truth, and these verses make me anxious.
4. ____ I feel I must change some areas of my life in preparation for His coming.
5. ____ I pray that Jesus will find me living as a faithful Christian when He returns.

Jesus Lived the Truth

Read Hebrews 4:15 in the margin. Meditate on the verse. Underline the words that most catch your attention.

If you think like me, you're probably most struck by the words "tempted in all things as we are, yet without sin." When most of us think of our temptations, it's difficult to imagine that Jesus faced the full range of our temptations. But in fact, we give in to temptations so quickly that we usually don't fully experience their power. Only Jesus—who faced the full brunt of temptation without ever sinning—can really understand its force. Still, He never failed.

As one who was fully God and fully human, Jesus *lived* the truth perfectly. Today, we can come to Him with confidence in times of need, knowing that He has walked where we walk and didn't fail.

Jesus and the Belt of Truth

The point of this lesson is simple: Jesus—who knew the truth, spoke the truth, and lived the truth—is still the Truth today. While the belt of truth entails more than simply knowing Him, we can't wear this piece of the armor without having a personal relationship with Jesus.

If you are not a believer, I encourage you to turn your life over to Christ, who paid for your sin and lives now to enable you to live a life of truth. Turn to "The ABCs of Salvation" on page 147. Pray, asking God to guide you to examine your life. If you are a believer, thank God and seek to live a life of integrity through His awesome and amazing power.

> "We do not have a high priest who cannot sympathize with our weaknesses, but One who has been tempted in all things as we are, yet without sin."
> *Hebrews 4:15, NASB*

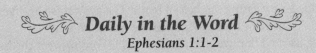

Daily in the Word
Ephesians 1:1-2

First-century authors typically placed greetings at the beginning so that the information was readily available as the scroll was first unrolled. The Book of Ephesians begins with a traditional first-century greeting which included the author's name, recipient's name, and a statement of blessing.

Beginning in verse 1, the author identified himself as Paul. He was no doubt a prisoner in Rome when he wrote this letter. The letter identifies the recipients as "the saints and believers in Christ Jesus at Ephesus" (v. 1).

Most likely, the letter was a circular letter that was distributed to believers in and around the city of Ephesus. Paul concluded his greeting by extending "grace" and "peace" to the reader. Paul used this greeting several times in his letters (Rom. 1:7; 1 Cor. 1:3; 2 Cor. 1:2).

APPLICATION
- Thank God for the Book of Ephesians, and ask Him to guide you as you read it.
- Thank God that we are saints and believers in Christ Jesus.

MEMORY VERSE FOR THIS WEEK
"Blessed be the God and Father of our Lord Jesus Christ, who has blessed us with every spiritual blessing in the heavens, in Christ." Ephesians 1:3

day  *four*

LIVING THE TRUTH

Put yourself in the middle of this story. You have been a Christian for 20 years. Several years ago, you were in your church's worship services when Jackie responded to Christ's call and was later baptized. Jackie has since studied God's Word, and she knows more about the Bible than you do.

Here's a question to begin this lesson: is it possible that Jackie is still not wearing the belt of truth?

❏ yes ❏ no ❏ uncertain

A follower of Jesus who knows His Word may not be faithfully living that Word—in which case Jackie isn't wearing the belt of truth. The answer is yes. Even a true believer can be disobedient to the Word that he or she knows.

In day 2 we learned that we must know God's Word to wear the belt of truth. Day 3 reminded us that knowing Jesus personally is essential to wearing the belt of truth. Day 4 will help you apply and live God's Word as faithful, committed followers of Christ. Through knowing Christ and His Word *and* living His Word, you will be wearing the belt of truth.

Jesus Is Our Model
Jesus grew up going to the synagoge where the words of the Old Testament scroll were read. Jesus responded to temptation by using the Word.

Read Matthew 4:1-11 and answer the following questions.

1. How many temptations did Jesus face? _____

2. How many times did the Devil quote Scripture? _____

3. What did the Devil offer to Jesus in the third temptation?

_____

4. How many times did Jesus quote Scripture? _____

5. Was Jesus victorious over the temptations? ❑ yes ❑ no

In these verses, we learn that the Devil tempted Jesus face-to-face. Matthew records three specific temptations, though it's possible that these three occurred at the end of many temptations (see Luke 4:1-13). Once the Devil even quoted Scripture in his attempt to lead Jesus astray.

Ultimately, he offered Jesus "all the kingdoms of the world" in return for His worship (Matt. 4:8). With each temptation, Jesus responded with the Word of God. Thus, the One who is the Word of God used the Word to make the right choices. Consequently, Jesus always made the right choices.

What do we learn from Jesus' temptation experience? **First, He made the right choices because His desire to please the Father was more important than anything the Enemy offered.** Jesus lived His life to do the Father's will (John 8:28-29), and nothing else mattered more to Him. He would even choose death over His own life, knowing the Father desired that choice (Luke 22:39-42). Can you see why the Enemy's offers to Jesus could not lure Him into sin? The Father meant more to Him than all the kingdoms of the world. How much do you want to please the Father? Does that desire help you say no to temptation?

Second, Jesus knew the Word sufficiently to respond to the Devil's attacks. Jesus quoted the Book of Deuteronomy three times! How many Christians know Deuteronomy that well? How many know the Scriptures in general that well?

Jesus treasured the Word in His heart (Ps. 119:11), and He used it immediately when He needed to refute the Enemy's offers. He didn't need a quick Scripture memorization course, nor did He need to find a scroll of Scriptures to quote the right verses. He simply knew the Word; He was ready for the attack.

I have a student who has a strong interest in Scripture memorization. Every day he carries his current memory verses in his pocket, and he studies them whenever possible. I've been with him at times when he faced trials, and he quoted the Word. I have seen him worried, and he turned to the Scriptures stored in his heart. I have no doubt that he quotes the Word when he faces personal temptation.

Do you know the Word that well? Do you have a strategic plan for Scripture memorization? If not, I hope you've started by learning the first phrase of this week's verse in "Daily in the Word." In the margin you will find steps to help you memorize God's Word. Follow these steps this week.

Third, Jesus experienced the Father's blessing when He overcame temptation. In fact, angels came and ministered to Him (Matt. 4:11). The best understanding suggests that they stayed with Him for a while. Perhaps He was exhausted from the fasting and the tempting. Maybe He was wrung out from the battle. Whatever Jesus' needs were, the Father sent angels to take care of Him.

Imagine the scene. One moment Jesus was face-to-face with the Devil, engaged in a grueling battle. But the next moment, the Devil disappeared and angels

STEPS FOR MEMORIZING THE WORD

1. Write the verse on a small card and carry it with you throughout the day.
2. Learn the text by memorizing one phrase at a time.
3. Meditate on the promise or help that you can personally receive by believing this verse.
4. Quote the verse throughout the day, considering how it will help you in spiritual warfare.
5. Ask someone to hold you accountable for your memorization.
6. Review, review, review.

appeared to comfort Him. The Father replaced His Son's pain of temptation with His divine comfort. Now, think about temptations in your life. Use the following activity to reflect on the feelings temptations produce.

Check (✔) the emotions you feel when you experience victory in temptation. Mark with an "x" each of the emotions you feel when you fail in temptation. Take a minute to compare the two.

____ fear	____ joy	____ excitement	____ peace
____ anger	____ pain	____ conviction	____ relief
____ love	____ shame	____ thankfulness	____ grief

Aren't the feelings of victory much better than those associated with defeat? When we know Jesus, know His Word, *and* live faithfully—that is, when we are truly wearing the belt of truth—we experience the genuine joy of Christian living. When you overcome temptation, look forward to God's blessing.

What We Do Is As Important As What We Don't Do

Paul's command to "put on the full armor of God" is a positive command; that is, he told us what *to do* rather than what *not* to do. That's the point of this entire study—if we do what God tells us to do by putting on the armor, we can stand against the Enemy.

Many view the Christian life as keeping a list of things to avoid. Christian living is indeed about fleeing temptation (1 Cor. 10:14; 2 Tim. 2:22), but it's also about doing good in order to avoid the sin that is "crouching at the door" (Gen. 4:7). James reminds us that if we know to do good and don't do it, that, too, is sin (Jas. 4:17).

Peter, preaching the gospel to Gentiles, summarized Jesus' ministry, saying, "He went about doing good and curing all who were under the tyranny of the Devil, because God was with Him" (Acts 10:38). Jesus stood against the Enemy not only by rejecting temptation but also by doing good that dislodged the Enemy's hold in people's lives. Perhaps if we focused more on doing good than on avoiding wrong, we would make more difference in our world.

Katherine Langford is a heroine of mine. Many years ago, she challenged me to read the book *In His Steps* by Charles M. Sheldon. It's the story of church members who decided to guide their lives by always asking, "What would Jesus do?" The book was the inspiration for the popular WWJD bracelets that Christian youth wore. These bracelets reminded the wearers that following Jesus means modeling the way He lived. As you continue this study, your commitment to know Jesus, know His Word, and live His Word will help you win the spiritual battles you face.

Circle each area in which your life needs to reflect the model Jesus left us. Ask God to help you with each area as you continue this study.

Bible reading	praying	giving
rejecting sin	serving	loving others
trusting God	fasting	witnessing

Perhaps if we focused more on doing good than on avoiding wrong, we would make more difference in our world.

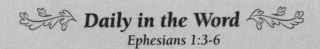

Daily in the Word
Ephesians 1:3-6

As we've learned before, the Book of Ephesians is divided into two major sections. Paul wrote the first three chapters of the book to help us understand what God has done for us and who we are in Christ. The last three chapters help us make application of this doctrinal reality.

Paul began the doctrinal section of the book by explaining the rich blessings God has poured out on those of us who are in Christ. First, Paul informed the Ephesians that God chose us to be "holy and blameless in His sight." Even though our lives are corrupted by sin, God amazingly sees us as clothed in the righteousness of His Son Jesus. Second, Paul showed that we have been "adopted through Jesus Christ for Himself" (v. 5). In spite of our rebellion, God chooses to lovingly call us His children. The spiritual blessings God bestows on us naturally lead to "the praise of His glorious grace" (v. 6).

APPLICATION
- Choose to be holy (set apart for His service).
- Praise God for His grace given to you. An acronym for grace is "God's Righteousness At Christ's Expense."

MEMORY VERSE FOR THIS WEEK
"Blessed be the God and Father of our Lord Jesus Christ, who has blessed us with every spiritual blessing in the heavens, in Christ." Ephesians 1:3

day  five

HOW WE LIVE TRUTH

I first heard the word *accountability* through a Promise Keepers group who wanted to help one another live holy lives. At the time, I thought that accountability would be a passing fad. Who would really want to talk to others about issues they face in their Christian lives?

Time has proven me wrong. In fact, I have since learned that the Bible expects believers to be accountable to others. In this lesson, our goal is to help you think about accountability as one way to make certain you're wearing the belt of truth.

What Is Accountability?

We define Christian accountability as "a willingness to be honest about, and to accept responsibility for, my actions as one means to strive for Christlike holiness." Notice these points about our definition:

- A person must desire to be held accountable. It is voluntary.
- Accountability requires honesty (hence, honest accountability connects to the belt of truth in this study).
- Accountability demands that we accept responsibility for our actions.
- Accountability isn't a shortcut allowing us to avoid spiritual disciplines such as Bible reading and prayer.
- The goal of accountability is growth in Christlikeness; personal holiness should be the result.

Why Should We Be Accountable to Someone?

Read Ephesians 6:10-14 and watch for the words "stand" or "stand firm." Paul strongly reminded his readers that they were in a spiritual battle against mighty powers—but they were to *stand* in this battle. Depending on the Bible translation that you use, you probably found the word "stand" three or four times in these verses. In fact, "stand" is the primary admonition in this passage. It pictures a soldier who stands in combat, doggedly opposing the Enemy.

The Lord who calls us to stand is the same One who strengthens us (Josh. 1:6-7,9; Eph. 6:10) so that we can stand. The prophet Isaiah foretold that the Messiah Himself would wear righteousness and truth around His waist (Isa. 11:5). God now gives us His armor for the battle—and the Enemy isn't strong enough to counter a believer who opposes him in God's armor.

At the same time, Paul assumed believers would fight together in the battle described in Ephesians 6. Indeed, much of Ephesians is about developing healthy relationships in the church, in the home, and in the workplace (2:11-22; 4:1–6:9). The church stands strongest against the Enemy when it stands united.

Believers encouraging one another in righteousness through intentional accountability is one way for the church to stand together (Heb. 10:24). When we have accountability partners, we know that we don't fight alone.

Where Is Accountability in the Bible?

Both the Old and New Testaments provide examples of one-on-one accountability relationships. In the Old Testament, we see the friendship of David and Jonathan; in the New Testament, great accountability among believers. Jesus sent out His messengers, expected a report from them, and corrected them when they missed the point of their ministry (Luke 10:1-20). He also taught church discipline that assumed accountability (Matt. 18:15-20). Paul demanded that the Corinthian church deal with sin in their midst rather than overlook it in arrogance (1 Cor. 5:1-5). The Thessalonians were to "admonish as a brother" those who did not obey Paul's instructions (2 Thess. 3:14-15, NASB). James instructed believers to confess their sins to one another (see Jas. 5:16 in margin).

The early church understood that they were a family, a body of believers knit together by their common bond in Christ. They met together and encouraged one another to love and do good works, knowing that a day of judgment would come (Heb. 10:23-27). Accountability in the early Church was a push toward righteousness. Most of us need that kind of push.

Check the statements below that best indicate your feelings about accountability.
- ❏ I am not willing to be accountable to anyone.
- ❏ I understand the need for accountability, but I am nervous about being held accountable.

> "Confess your sins to one another and pray for one another, so that you may be healed. The intense prayer of the righteous is very powerful."
> *James 5:16*

❏ I have an accountability partner, but this process is not helping me
   to be more faithful to Christ.
❏ I am willing to give accountability a try, but with great hesitation.
❏ I am ready to have an accountability partner.
❏ I have an accountability partner. Our relationship helps me grow
   as a Christian.

How Does Accountability Relate to the Belt of Truth?

The answer to this question is simple: good accountability keeps us honest.
I am a professor of evangelism, but that doesn't mean I'm naturally an evangelist.
Rather, I'm introverted enough that sometimes I struggle to witness to others. I
wish that lost persons would just come to me and say, "I hear you're a professor.
Would you please tell me how to follow Jesus?" Needless to say, that has never
happened! I realize that I must initiate most evangelistic encounters, and I've
learned that I do that best when I'm held accountable to that important task.

   Twice each month, my accountability partner asks me about my evangelism.
He keeps me honest and pushes me toward obedience—both essential to wearing
the belt of truth. I do more evangelism because I want to be a person of integrity
before God, my accountability partner, my family, and my students. I want to be
wearing the belt of truth.

> **On a scale of 1-5 with 1 being not at all and 5 being completely,
> rate your level of obedience in your Christian walk before each
> of these groups:**
>
> _____ coworkers or classmates
> _____ church members
> _____ neighbors
> _____ family

   If you are less than honest in some areas of your life, accountability may
strengthen your Christian walk. Take time to ask God about His direction
regarding your accountability.

What Are Some Guidelines for Accountability?

These simple guidelines for accountability may help you. Be sure to ask God
for His direction.

   1. For this study, seek a partner (or partners) who will hold you account-
      able primarily to the spiritual disciplines of the armor of God.
   2. In many cases, the best accountability partner for spiritual disciplines
      is a Christian spouse.
   3. Other than your spouse, never have an accountability partner of the
      opposite sex.
   4. Determine a time to meet. I suggest no less than every other week.
   5. Determine a set series of questions to ask one another. At this point
      in this study, questions such as these are appropriate:
      • Have you read the Bible daily?
      • What have you learned from God's Word this week?
      • What have you learned about knowing Jesus this week?
      • Is there an area of life where you aren't obedient?
      • How may I specifically pray for you?

6. Be honest in all responses. Accountability should foster integrity, not lying.
7. Don't gossip about information shared in an accountability session.
8. Commit yourself to strive for growth and holiness. Set goals to help you grow in Christ.
9. Don't allow each other to give up. Push one another to do well (Heb. 10:24).
10. Commit to pray for one another every day.

Perhaps someone in your study group would be willing to be your accountability partner during this study. Seek God's direction and take the steps necessary to seek encouragement as you wear the belt of truth.

A Review: Wearing the Full Armor of God

Wearing the belt of truth means knowing Jesus, knowing His Word, and living that Word. As we will see in the following weeks, this piece of the armor is directly related to the rest of the armor—as all of the pieces are interconnected. To help you see that truth, the first page of each new week includes a fill-in-the-blank review of all of the armor of God. I hope that these sections will help you to remember the armor. More importantly, I pray that you'll wear that armor!

Key Definition
Redemption—a payment used to set someone free.

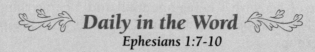

Daily in the Word
Ephesians 1:7-10

Paul continued to speak about the abundance of spiritual blessings that God pours out on those who are in Christ. The primary blessing is redemption made possible "through His blood" (v. 7). The term *redemption* was commonly used to speak of a payment made to set a slave or prisoner free.

Through the blood of Christ, we are forgiven for our trespasses and freed from the penalty and bondage of sin. This Scripture teaches us that our spiritual freedom did not come cheaply; rather, the death of Christ made our redemption. God now lavishes His grace on us, and He will fulfill His eternal plan in Christ. All creatures, both in heaven and on earth, will ultimately bow before Him.

APPLICATION
- Thank God that He has redeemed you.
- Because your spiritual freedom didn't come cheaply, stay close to Jesus and live His Word to win over temptation.

MEMORY VERSE FOR THIS WEEK
"Blessed be the God and Father of our Lord Jesus Christ, who has blessed us with every spiritual blessing in the heavens, in Christ."
Ephesians 1:3

---

1. William Hendricksen, *Exposition of the Gospel According to John* in *New Testament Commentary* (Grand Rapids: Baker, 1953), 268.

The following activity will be completed in your group session.

Who Do You Say I Am?

For each false statement 1) choose which of Satan's schemes leads to this statement, 2) find Scriptures that prove this statement isn't biblical, and 3) name which of Christ's identities shows that it's false.

FALSE STATEMENT	SATAN'S SCHEME	SCRIPTURE(S)	CHRIST'S IDENTITY
1. Jesus is only one of the many routes to God.	If Satan can keep us on some other path, he keeps us from the only way to salvation.	John 14:6, Acts 4:12	The Way
2. Jesus couldn't have possibly been born of a virgin.			
3. Jesus must have committed some sin during His lifetime.			
4. Jesus was a great prophet, but He was no more than that.			
5. Jesus died as a martyr, but He didn't die for the sins of the world.			
6. Jesus' bodily resurrection was only a myth propagated by the disciples.			

The Breastplate of Righteousness

Ed and Ann Miller's second son, Al, graduated from high school last year. Uncertain what to study in college, he decided instead to get a job and remain at home for the next year. He also decided that as an adult, he had the right to choose whether or not to attend church—and he chose not to go.

His parents grieve his decision, but how can they force a 19-year-old to attend church with them? They've told him about the church, the bride of Christ, and its importance in God's kingdom, but their admonition hasn't helped. Now, they can only pray that Al will reject the Enemy's enticement and make good choices.

Did Ed and Ann make the right decision? Is Al being misled by the Enemy? How might his parents help him make the right decision? In week 2, we'll learn what it means to wear the breastplate of righteousness in order to defeat the Enemy in our lives. We will learn that wearing the breastplate means making right decisions when faced with temptation.

REVIEWING THE FULL ARMOR OF GOD

Belt of _____
- Know Jesus
- Know His Word
- Live the Word

day one

RIGHTEOUSNESS: LIVING LIKE JESUS

Pastor Glenn's sermon series on Ephesians 6 was going well. His church had rarely seen him as excited as he was to preach on the breastplate of righteousness. He thoroughly described the breastplate of a Roman soldier. "Sometimes the Roman soldier's breastplate didn't cover his back," he told the congregation, "because no good soldier would turn and run." Some breastplates did, in fact, cover the back, but the pastor nevertheless concluded his message with a fervent plea. "We cannot turn in defeat and run from this battle with the Enemy."

While Pastor Glenn communicated the challenge (not to run in defeat), he failed to help his church know *how* to wear the breastplate. They knew more about what this piece of armor looked like in the first century than what it means for us today. Wearing the breastplate of righteousness means that we live like Jesus did—a life of obedience to the Father's will.

Jesus Is Our Model of Righteousness

Read the verses from 1 John in the margin. As you can see, John felt passionately about the importance of righteousness. In fact, he emphasized our call to the righteousness of Jesus—our standard of righteousness. How do we live up to Jesus' standard? All of us are sinners (Rom. 3:23), and none of us is good (Mark 10:18). In our sinful state, we are spiritually dead (Eph. 2:1-3). Nothing we can do makes us righteous in God's eyes. On our own, we're simply in deep trouble.

But—and here's the good news—God gives us *His* righteousness when we become believers. Theologians use the word *impute* to describe the process by which God attributes to us that which we can't possess ourselves. We can't be righteous, so God makes us righteous in His eyes through the death of Jesus, who paid our debt of sin in full. The Apostle Paul described the process this way:

"Just as through one man's [Adam's] disobedience the many were made sinners, so also through the one man's [Jesus'] obedience the many will be made righteous" (Rom. 5: 19).

"He made the One who did not know sin to be sin for us, so that we might become the righteousness of God in Him" (2 Cor. 5:21).

If God makes us righteous, do we really need to worry about the way we live? Does it really matter if we wear the breastplate of righteousness? Paul answered that question, too, by writing, "What should we say then? Should we continue in sin in order that grace may multiply? Absolutely not!" (Rom. 6:1-2).

That's precisely the point of wearing the breastplate of righteousness. We who have been saved and made righteous by God's grace must daily choose to make righteous choices. God gives us His armor *so that* we can live the way He expects us to live: like Jesus did. To do that, we need to think about Jesus' life.

List below words or phrases that you believe describe how Jesus lived. Be prepared to discuss your answers with your group.

_____

_____

Jesus Focused on Pleasing the Father

We discussed Jesus' focus in week 1, so this observation isn't new to you. Jesus demonstrated His obedience to the Father when Satan tempted Him in the

"If anyone does sin, we have an advocate with the Father—Jesus Christ the righteous One." *1 John 2:1*

"If you know that He is righteous, you know this as well: everyone who does what is right has been born of Him." *1 John 2:29*

"Little children, let no one deceive you! The one who does what is right is righteous, just as He is righteous." *1 John 3:7*

Key Definition
Impute—To credit to a person an attribute; ascribe

Daily choose to make righteous choices.

27

wilderness. However, I want to emphasize it again: the Son of God (our model for righteousness) always focused on pleasing the Father.

Read the following Scriptures, and underline the words that demonstrate Jesus' focus on His Father.

I do nothing on My own. But just as the Father taught Me, I say these things. The One who sent Me is with Me. He has not left Me alone, because I always do what pleases Him (John 8:28-29).

He said, "Abba, Father! All things are possible for You. Take this cup away from Me. Nevertheless, not what I will, but what You will" (Mark 14:36).

I have not spoken on My own, but the Father Himself who sent Me has given Me a command as to what I should say and what I should speak. … I speak just as the Father has told Me (John 12:49-50).

Jesus called out with a loud voice, "Father, into Your hands I entrust My Spirit" (Luke 23:46).

Above everything else, Jesus simply trusted His Father and desired to do His will. For us to wear the breastplate of righteousness, we must do the same.

What are some self-serving reasons for being obedient to God? You don't want to get caught? You're afraid of being judged by God? You don't want to embarrass your family? You're a leader in your church? You're worried about the consequences? All of these may be legitimate motivations for making righteous choices, but they're not the best motivation, which is simply to please the Father as Jesus did.

Do you really want to please the Father above everything else?
❏ yes ❏ no ❏ sometimes

Spend a few minutes in honest prayer right now.

Jesus Would Not Be Disobedient

One of my students likes to hunt deer. He told me about his first season, which included many hours in the woods with nothing to show for it but plenty of birds and squirrels. One morning while sitting in the stand, he heard leaves rustling behind him. The sound finally grew so loud that he turned to see what those pesky squirrels were doing. To his surprise, a deer was within 10 yards of his stand, and he hadn't even picked up his gun. As you may have guessed, the deer was startled by the movement and ran into the woods. He said afterward, "I missed my opportunity because I didn't stay focused on my goal."

Jesus came to earth with a clear goal: to seek and to save the lost (Luke 19:10), fulfilling the Father's will that He would "save His people from their sins" (Matt. 1:21). But even Christ faced potential distractions from His goal. Even the good we do can keep us from God's best. God may have already shown you a distraction that limits your ability to serve Him first. Listen for God's voice as you make daily choices.

Match each text with the potential distraction Jesus faced.

1. ____ Matthew 16:21-23   A. The crowds wanted Him
                                to be their king.

2. ____ Mark 14:32-36   B. Facing death on the cross
                                was horrible.

3. ____ Luke 4:5-7   C. Peter didn't want Him to die.

4. ____ John 6:14-15   D. The Enemy offered Him the world.

Think about it. The Enemy offered Jesus all of the kingdoms of the world. Jesus could easily have been crowned an earthly king. The thoughts of the cross were painful. Even Peter challenged Him when He talked about dying. Jesus might have gained a kingdom while avoiding the pain of the cross, encouraged by both the crowds and His disciples. Would that route have been inviting to you?

Not so for Jesus. The battles He faced were intense, but He wouldn't be detoured from His chosen path. Nothing in this world would deflect His attention from the Father's will. Wearing the breastplate of righteousness means allowing nothing to get in the way of our living out the righteousness God has already given us.

> Wearing the breastplate of righteousness means allowing nothing to get in the way of our living out the righteousness God has already given us.

Circle the obstacles that sometimes keep you from doing all God expects from you.

entertainment	pride	peer pressure	selfishness
friends	anger	Internet	family needs
money	work	fear	too little fear

other _____

If we choose to wear the breastplate of righteousness, we must confront the distractions and obstacles we face. If your obstacles are too little knowledge or training, ask your pastor about training opportunities your church will offer when this study ends. For other issues, ask your accountability partner to help you address each one so that you can stay focused on godly obedience. Remember, we put on the armor with the help of other believers.

What do you sense God is asking you to avoid or stop doing? Write your answer in the margin. Then complete this prayer.

God, I want to live a holy life … _____

_____

_____

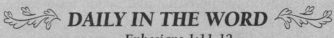
In these verses, Paul likely spoke of Jewish believers who had believed in the Messiah prior to the Gentiles. God had ordained them to believe in Him first, but their belief was not to be a source of pride. They believed only because God had ordained it, and "bring[ing] praise to His glory" was the intended result (v. 12).

The primary spiritual blessing that Paul spoke of in verses 11-12 is *inheritance*— that is, that God has graciously made us His heirs. As a loving Father, He has written us into His will. God not only gives us blessings in the present, but He also guarantees blessings in the future. All He has promised will come to pass because He "works out everything in agreement with the decision of His will" (v. 11).

APPLICATION
- Thank God that He has included you as His heir.
- Meditate on the reality of heaven—a promised place that will come to pass.

MEMORY VERSE FOR THIS WEEK
"I pray that the God of our Lord Jesus Christ, the glorious Father, would give you a spirit of wisdom and revelation in the knowledge of Him." Ephesians 1:17

Answers to activity on page 29: 1. C; 2. B; 3. D; 4. A

God not only gives us blessings in the present, but He also guarantees blessings in the future.

day two

THE ENEMY ATTACKS RIGHTEOUSNESS

While teaching a lesson on Christian living, the minister to students told his group, "On your sheet of paper, write the two most important questions you want to ask me." The students wrote quickly. "How do we know Christianity is right?" asked one student. Another asked, "Why is it wrong to have sex with somebody you love?" Most of the questions, though, sounded something like this one from Tom, a senior-high leader: "How do I keep from doing wrong? I want to live right, but I fail so many times."

Tom was learning that wearing the breastplate of righteousness isn't easy because Satan continually works to lead us into unrighteousness. All of us struggle against three common enemies: the world, our sinful nature (the flesh), and the

All of us struggle against three common enemies.

Devil (Eph. 2:1-2). Because the world itself is distorted by sin and we have a natural inclination to sin, the Devil seeks to lead us to fail. He doesn't want us to live obediently, become more like Jesus, or be righteous.

In day 2 we'll examine some of the strategies Satan uses to lure us into temptation. Through our examination, we want to understand better what it means to wear the breastplate of righteousness. This lesson focuses on the story of Adam and Eve.[1]

Strategy 1—The Enemy Begins a Conversation with Us

Read Genesis 3:1-7 in your Bible. The snake in the garden of Eden is later called "the great dragon ... the ancient serpent, who is called the Devil and Satan" (Rev. 12:9). That Enemy, craftier than any other animal in the garden, somehow grabbed Eve's attention and began a conversation with her.

In the course of that conversation, Satan questioned God's Word (Gen. 3:1), blatantly denied God's Word (v. 4), and challenged God's character (v. 5). The conversation ultimately led to Eve's choice to eat from the forbidden tree (v. 6).

Though we don't know for certain all that happened in that garden, with hindsight we can agree that Eve's first mistake was entering into a conversation with the Devil. He is sly, conniving, evil, and yet convincing. We are no match for him in our own power.

Of course, we don't speak directly with the physical and visible serpent as Eve did, but have you ever entertained a conversation with the Devil like this one?

- "Go ahead, it won't hurt you just this once."
- ✳ "But I shouldn't do it ... although you're right, it probably won't hurt me. And at least it will hurt only me, if anybody."
- "That's right. And besides, no one will know."
- ✳ "I probably can hide it, and think about the pleasure it will bring me."
- "Yeah, just think about the pleasure it will bring. I wouldn't offer it to you unless it would be fun. Just think what you'll be missing."
- ✳ "Just think what I'll be missing."

And the conversation goes on until we decide to give in to the temptation. Get this: *the longer we discuss the temptation with the serpent, the more likely we will give in and sin.* The more we think about the temptation, the closer we get to failure.

Simply resisting the urge to join the Enemy in conversation isn't enough; we must resist by submitting to God (Jas. 4:7). We need to flee temptation by running directly to God and putting on His armor. The breastplate of righteousness that God gives us triumphantly deflects the Enemy's arrows.

> The more we think about the temptation, the closer we get to failure.

We are all guilty of listening too much to the Devil's reasoning. Do any of these statements remind you of Eve's conversation? Check (✔) each of the following excuses that you have used to convince yourself to give in to temptation:

- ❑ "God really wouldn't want me to miss out on this fun."
- ❑ "If I commit this sin, nobody else will get hurt."
- ❑ "Nobody else will find out about this sin."
- ❑ "I know God loves me, and He will forgive me again."
- ❑ "Maybe it's not really a sin. Maybe I'm just being too legalistic."
- ❑ Other: _____

Strategy 2—The Enemy Directs Our Attention to What We're Missing

Review Genesis 3:1-7. God had given Adam and Eve access to all of the trees of the garden, warning them, however, not to eat of the tree of knowledge of good and evil (Gen. 2:16-17). He made more than adequate provision for them, but the serpent directed them to *what they were missing*. The serpent said God was only keeping the tree from Adam and Eve because He didn't want them to be like Him.

Think about advertising strategies. Don't they most often lead us to focus on what we don't have? There's a great new car on the road, and you can have one— but you don't have it yet. If you drink this drink, you'll have an exciting life with friends and beautiful women—but you don't have it yet. Advertisers get us to see the voids in our lives, not the current blessings. Satan was a great advertising agent.

When we focus our attention on what we don't have, we place ourselves in a dangerous place of temptation. We don't have what others have, so we greedily covet, breaking one of God's specific commandments (Ex. 20:17). A desire for someone we don't have drives us to lust. Even worry is a similar sin—we get so caught up in what we can't control that we lose our focus on God's provision (Matt. 6:25-34). If we would remember that the Father makes adequate provision for all of our needs, we wouldn't need to focus on what we think we're missing. We would be less susceptible to many temptations. In fact, if we really believed that God is all we need, the Enemy's temptations would be less inviting. Remember, *His* armor, not ours, defeats the Enemy.

> **Focus now on God's blessings for you, not on what you're missing. Take two minutes and list all of the blessings that come to mind. When you complete your list, thank God for His goodness.**

\

\

Strategy 3—The Enemy Makes Sin Look Good

Adam and Eve saw that the forbidden tree "was good for food and delightful to look at, and … desirable for obtaining wisdom" (Gen. 3:6). The fruit appealed to their physical desires and seemingly offered knowledge they didn't have. The "lust of the flesh and the lust of the eyes and the boastful pride of life" (1 John 2:16, NASB) caught Adam and Eve—not unlike how we're trapped by the same desires.

Let's be honest. Most of the time we sin because sin looks good to us. Like a hunter who lures with bait that hides its deadly consequences, Satan makes sin look inviting. In fact, sin can be fun—but only for a time (Heb. 11:25).

In the desert the Hebrews worshiped a golden calf and then engaged in partying and sexual sin (Ex. 32:2-6). It wasn't long, however, before God judged His people and ended their immoral "fun." The idol worshipers received a plague for their punishment (Ex. 32:35).

Likewise, the prodigal son must have been lured by the exciting prospects of living a life of luxury, and he probably had a good time as he "squandered his estate in foolish living" (Luke 15:13). In the end, though, he found himself a hired servant in a pigpen (Luke 15:15).

Unfortunately, we focus on temporary fun while ignoring sin's long-term consequences. Satan offers us the world, but he wants us to ignore the cost of worshiping him (Matt. 4:8-10). Sin looks so inviting. Regrettably, the process of temptation too often ends with our wrong choices. Are you easy prey for the Enemy?

Believers who are wearing the breastplate of righteousness understand that we must take each of the following steps when we face temptation. Check (✔) the easiest step for you, and then put an "x" by the step that is most difficult for you. Ask God to help you take each step when you face temptation this week.

1. _____ Run to God in prayer. When the Devil wants you to enter into conversation with him, choose instead to talk to God.
2. _____ Focus on God's goodness and blessings. When the Devil entices you to see what you're missing, think about the cross.
3. _____ Remember the consequences of sin. Think past the temporary pleasure to recognize the long-term pain of disobedience.
4. _____ Say no to the Devil's offer.
5. _____ When He has given you strength to defeat the Enemy, be sure to thank God for giving you His breastplate of righteousness.

More In-Depth Study

Using a Bible dictionary, study the word *temptation*. In many cases in the Bible, the same root word for temptation is translated as "test." How do you think a temptation and a test are different? Be prepared to discuss this with your small group.

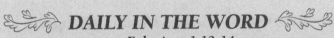

DAILY IN THE WORD
Ephesians 1:13-14

Day 1's Bible reading revealed that God has predestined an inheritance He will give to those who are in Christ, beginning with the early Jewish believers. In today's reading Paul recognized Gentile believers who also "heard the word of truth" (v. 13). They heard the gospel, believed, and were "sealed with the promised Holy Spirit" (v. 13). The Spirit of God in them was their "down payment" for the eternal blessing God had guaranteed (v. 14). They, too, like us, were God's heirs.

As you conclude this section on spiritual blessings, notice the condition on which these blessings are given. Paul reminded his readers 13 times in 12 verses that these blessings are available only "in" or "through" Jesus Christ. We are chosen, adopted, redeemed, forgiven, and sealed—but only through Him.

APPLICATION
• Think about what it means to be adopted by God.
• Listen closely to God's Spirit who seals you and guides you.

day  *three*

RUNNING FROM TEMPTATION

During testimony time at a local church, one member stood and told of God's grace to her husband who had just become a believer. Another explained how God provided for his family's medical costs. A third member rose and could hardly speak. Emotion overcame her as she tenderly told about God's presence surrounding her beloved mother's recent death.

Then a fourth member stood to speak. "I thank God," he said, "because I have found victory over sin. I used to battle against temptation, but now I know what victory is." He concluded his testimony with, "And really, I don't even have temptations anymore."

If that's where you are—more holy than Jesus, who faced temptations until He died—then you probably don't need to study the remaining days of this week. I suspect, of course, that most of you will continue studying. Day 3 demonstrates how wearing the breastplate of righteousness helps you stand against the Enemy's temptations. The story of Joseph's defense against the lures of Potiphar's wife illustrates this point.

Wearing the Breastplate Means Thinking Properly

Read the story of Joseph and Potiphar's wife in Genesis 39:1-23.

To put it simply, Mrs. Potiphar wanted to sleep with Joseph, and she aggressively chased him. Think about the situation that confronted Joseph:
- He was a young, good-looking man (39:6) with natural sexual desires, and she was the older wife of an important leader in Egypt.
- Joseph lived far from his family and thus far from accountability.
- Mrs. Potiphar tempted him every day, and even the best of men might eventually weaken under such advances.
- Surely she sought him when no one was around, and they could hide the indiscretion.
- God blessed Potiphar because of Joseph's presence in his home (39:4-5); maybe Joseph "deserved" this reward for his services.

A young man with an older woman who was the aggressor—who could blame Joseph if he followed her lead? Add up all of these possible excuses, and we might be tempted to overlook Joseph's sin (albeit wrongly) had he given in to this woman.

Look closely, though, at the first three words of Genesis 39:8: "but he refused." This action influenced the rest of Joseph's life (though it first landed him in prison!). Behind his refusal were these thoughts: sleeping with this woman would be a betrayal of his master's trust, an offense against his master, and a sin against God. He knew that such actions would be "great evil" (v. 9). Joseph also counted the cost of his own self-respect and moral purity.

Wearing the breastplate of righteousness helps us know the difference between right and wrong. If we think wrongly—if we misdefine what sin is and what it's not—we're much more likely to act wrongly. If Joseph had *thought* that adultery wasn't wrong, he would have easily given in to Potiphar's wife. He *knew*, though, that she was off-limits to him (v. 9).

Check (✔) any of these statements that reflect your thinking when you face a temptation.

❑ Perhaps this sin isn't so wrong after all.
❑ Everyone else is doing it, so it must be OK.
❑ I'm not sure if this thought is right or wrong.
❑ I know this action is probably sinful, but I'll most likely do it anyway.
❑ I know this action is wrong, so I must reject the temptation.
❑ I think differently with each temptation. Who knows what I will choose?
❑ If I *really* want to give in, I'll probably convince myself that this action is OK.
❑ Actually, I haven't considered how I think when facing a temptation.

Wearing the Breastplate Means Choosing to Do Right

To wear the breastplate of righteousness, we must engage in right thinking. Yet, don't we sometimes make poor choices even when we know that our actions are wrong? If so, thinking properly is not the *only* step needed.

Read Genesis 39:10 in the margin. This verse shows us much about the temptation process that Joseph faced. The Enemy continues to use the same process with us today as he did with Joseph.

First, Potiphar's wife was relentless in her temptations. She refused to take Joseph's rejection as final. Surely she thought, "He will *eventually* give in."

Second, the text suggests that Potiphar's wife had an intentional strategy. The first step was to get Joseph only to "lie beside her," perhaps to make him more comfortable with the next possible step—to "be with her." The Enemy offers us little compromises that lead to greater sin. "It's OK to watch an R-rated movie on TV," Satan says. "After all, that may help me lead you into Internet pornography."

Third, the verse implies the potential power of evil words. Surely Mrs. Potiphar used more than words, but her words must have been potent as well. We know that her invitation was obvious—"lie with me"—but we can only imagine what else she said to Joseph to grab his attention. Seductive words are powerful!

Fourth, we can imagine Mrs. Potiphar's appearance on these occasions. A little too much flesh? What's too much? As an old saying goes, "If you've got it, flaunt it." Few remember that causing someone to sin by your immodesty is also your sin.

Nevertheless, Joseph rejected the advances of Mrs. Potiphar and chose to do right. His master had trusted him with his household, and Joseph wouldn't betray his master's trust. More specifically, he wouldn't sin against God (Gen. 39:9). Like

"As she spoke to Joseph day after day, he did not listen to her to lie beside her or be with her."
Genesis 39:10, NASB

David later, Joseph understood that his sin against Potiphar would offend his Creator as well (Ps. 51:4). Think about how Joseph's process for making this right choice might have looked.

"If I give in to her advances, the consequences are ..."

Positive +	Negative −
I will have temporary sexual pleasure.	I will break my master's trust.
	My master will be angry.
	I will sin against God.
	My conscience will feel guilty.

"If I reject her advances, the consequences are ..."

Positive +	Negative −
My master will still trust me.	I will miss temporary sexual pleasure.
God will be pleased.	
My conscience will be clear.	

Viewing Joseph's decision this way shows us that the pleasures of disobedience weren't worth the negative consequences, and the positive results of obedience mattered much more than the temporary excitement of disobedience. Joseph made the right choice *because he kept the right perspective*.

> **Based on your study of Joseph's life, state two reasons you can use to reject sin the next time you face a temptation.**

1. _____

2. _____

Wearing the Breastplate Means Fleeing Temptation

Mrs. Potiphar didn't give up easily. At a time when she and Joseph were alone in the house, she again tempted him. She grabbed his cloak, he fled, and she then accused him of attempting to have sex with her (Gen. 39:11-14). Potiphar imprisoned Joseph under these false pretenses, but God later used that imprisonment to raise Joseph to a significant position of leadership in Egypt (Gen. 39:19–41:57).

The point is that Joseph intentionally ran as fast as he could from the temptation. Seldom do we think of "wearing armor" and "fleeing" together, but the two concepts become a unit in this story. Joseph wore the breastplate of righteousness by fleeing temptation (see 2 Tim. 2:22).

Paul reminded us that God provides a way out of every temptation (1 Cor. 10:13). Sometimes the way out that God provides is two feet that allow us to *run* in the opposite direction! Too often, though, we linger around temptation. We want to get close enough to the sin to taste it, all the while hoping that we won't give in to the temptation—and then we wonder why we fail. Learn from Joseph how to wear the breastplate of righteousness by fleeing.

Sometimes the way out that God provides is two feet that allow us to *run* in the opposite direction!

36

A word of caution: In what seems to have been an unusual situation, no one else was in the house when Potiphar's wife accused Joseph of rape. In the "he said, she said" battle that followed, Joseph lost. How careful do we need to be to avoid situations where we could be accused of sin—even wrongly and unfairly? No wonder we need to avoid even the appearance of evil (see 1 Thess. 5:22 in the margin).

"Abstain from all appearance of evil."
1 Thessalonians 5:22, KJV

DAILY IN THE WORD
Ephesians 1:15-19

In these verses, Paul demonstrated his love for the Christians in the area of Ephesus through the intercessory prayers he offered on their behalf. Paul's primary concern was that they know and understand God. He prayed that they would understand that God calls us to Him, rejoices over us as His inheritance, and gives us His power by which to live. The mention of "power" here introduces a theme found throughout Ephesians. In this text, Paul focused on God's power, available to all believers. God gives us immeasurable power according to the strength of His might! Who can defeat those who are in Christ?

APPLICATION
  • Pray today for someone who needs to know more about God.
  • Reflect on this thought today: "Nothing can defeat me if I live in Christ's power."

MEMORY VERSE FOR THIS WEEK
"I pray that the God of our Lord Jesus Christ, the glorious Father, would give you a spirit of wisdom and revelation in the knowledge of Him." Ephesians 1:17

day *four*

STANDING AGAINST TEMPTATION

Chris, a church member, faced many years of struggle with drug addiction. He said his parents were the cause of his addiction. Then he said his girlfriend contributed to his problem. The government, too, shared the blame because they didn't give him enough help in jail to really get rid of the habit. Eventually the church was responsible for not teaching him about the effects of drug abuse. Church members tried to help Chris, but he refused to take responsibility for his actions.

Before we judge Chris too harshly, let's remember that we sometimes easily give in to sin—and our excuses are numerous. Yesterday we studied an episode in the life of Joseph, who made a righteous choice in the face of strong temptation. Not all of us, though, are so strong. Think about why we so easily give in to temptation.

Here are some common reasons that explain why we fail when tempted. Rank them in the order of occurrence, using "1" for what you believe is the most common excuse that people give.

_____ We really don't think we'll get caught.
_____ We don't see our actions as sin.
_____ We give in too easily to peer pressure.
_____ The world makes sin look inviting.
_____ We don't think we'll face any consequences for our actions.
_____ Other: _____

Today we'll view the breastplate of righteousness from a negative experience—from the perspective of a biblical character who made an unrighteous choice when tempted. Through the story of David and Bathsheba, we'll learn about the dangers of choosing not to walk in righteousness. Specifically, we will study the cycle of sin that marked David's actions.

Even a Man of God Can Fail

When Stephen defended his faith in Acts 7, he noted that David "found favor in God's sight" (7:46). Even more significantly, God called David "a man after His own heart" (1 Sam. 13:14, NASB). We might think that a man with such a glowing résumé wouldn't fail miserably when faced with temptation. But you will see otherwise as we look at David's adultery with Bathsheba.

David reminds each of us we're one bad decision away from falling into unrighteousness. Even someone chosen by God to lead His people can commit a sin such as adultery. "Put on the full armor of God" therefore declares more than just a phrase in a first-century letter. We should put on the armor to protect us from the sin that could so easily grab each of us (Heb. 12:1).

Reflect on the truth that even David could fall into grave sin. Underline two or three words that describe your feelings when your own bad decisions caused negative consequences.

fear	sorrow	remorse	shame
guilt	loss	hopelessness	anger

David Allowed His Humanity to Lead Him

Read 2 Samuel 11:1-4, looking closely at David's actions.

From the vantage of walking on his roof (a common activity on flat-roofed homes in the ancient world), David saw a beautiful woman bathing. Aroused and curious, he sought information about her. What he learned about her was significant. She was Bathsheba, "the daughter of one of David's best fighters (Eliab—2 Sam. 23:34), the granddaughter of his most trusted counselor (Ahitophel—2 Sam. 16:23; 23:34), and the wife of one of his inner circle of honored soldiers (Uriah—2 Sam. 23:39)."[2]

Simple reasoning would suggest to us that if David really wanted to commit adultery, Bathsheba wasn't the wisest choice. Too many other relationships were at risk, and too many of David's loyal followers would be hurt. Most importantly, God would judge his actions.

Apparently David didn't allow reasoning to lead him. He saw Bathsheba, wanted her, sent for her, and slept with her—failing to consider the consequences. Knowing who she was, yet driven by his sexual desires, he committed adultery with her. At least briefly, his breastplate of righteousness was nowhere to be found.

Compare David's situation to Joseph's situation in day 3's study.

How were their situations alike?

_____

How were their situations different?

_____

How did relationships factor into their final decisions?

_____

David failed when he allowed his hormones to lead, whereas Joseph followed God. What leads you when you choose to sin? Sometimes our hormones lead us, and we seek pleasure in immoral ways. At times our emotions such as anger and bitterness control us. At other times our need for approval drives us to compromise our morals in order to be accepted. Sometimes a drive for wealth leads us astray. Whatever wrongly leads us, we know that we aren't wearing the breastplate of righteousness unless we are led by God's Spirit.

David Tried to Cover Up His Sin

David's actions with Bathsheba resulted in her becoming pregnant (2 Sam. 11:5). Quickly, David attempted to conceal his sin.

According to 2 Samuel 11:6-17, how did David try to hide his sin?

vv. 6-11 _____

_____

vv. 12-13 _____

_____

vv. 14-17 _____

_____

Your responses probably show that David's cover-up required more and more effort and led him to deeper and deeper sin. When we try to hide our sins, this reality prevails. Keeping your sins hidden typically requires an exhausting amount of effort.

David called Uriah home from battle, trusting that he would sleep with his wife and thus be considered the baby's father. When that didn't work, David got Uriah drunk, again assuming that he would go home to his wife in his drunken state.

Ultimately, David set up Uriah for death. With Uriah out of the way, David married Bathsheba (2 Sam. 11:27).

Contrast Uriah's response to David's actions. Uriah wouldn't sleep with his wife while his commander and colleagues were encamped in the fields, fighting for Israel. Even drunkenness would not lead him to compromise his commitment. The pleasure of being with his wife would have to wait. Loyalty ruled over pleasure. Meanwhile, for David, pleasure ruled over all.

Here is a basic rule of spiritual warfare: the Enemy works in hiddenness. He led Adam and Eve to sin, and they hid themselves in their shame (Gen. 3:8). Joseph's brothers tried to cover up their sin when they sold him into slavery (Gen. 37:18-36). Ananias and Sapphira hid their sin in their hearts until Peter confronted them (Acts 5:1-10). And today we, too, hide our sins.

On the other hand, we wear the breastplate of righteousness publicly. Though many of our righteous acts are personal and unseen, we can't wear this piece of the armor without others seeing our good works that please the Father (Matt. 5:16). Wearing the breastplate enables us to live righteously so that we have nothing to hide. If you know you will need to hide your actions, you know you're not wearing the breastplate of righteousness. Think before you act!

> *Here is a basic rule of spiritual warfare: the Enemy works in hiddenness.*

The Good News: God Did Not Give Up on David

Second Samuel 11:27 summarizes God's response to David's actions: "The LORD considered what David had done to be evil." If the story ended here, this would be one of the most tragic stories in the Bible. But look at the very next words: "So the LORD sent Nathan to David" (2 Sam. 12:1).

God didn't leave David alone; instead, He sent him a prophet whose words brought David to confession and repentance (2 Sam. 12:1-15; Ps. 51). Though God didn't remove all of the consequences of David's sin—the baby born as a result of the affair died—He mercifully did not require David's death as judgment for his actions (Lev. 20:10; 24:17).

The good news for us is that God graciously gives us new opportunities to put on the breastplate of righteousness. If you need to renew your commitment to wearing the breastplate, conclude today's lesson by praying these words of David:

> Be gracious to me, God,
> according to Your faithful love;
> according to Your abundant compassion,
> blot out my rebellion.
> Wash away my guilt,
> and cleanse me from my sin.
> God, create a clean heart for me
> and renew a steadfast spirit within me.
>
> Psalm 51:1-2,10

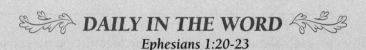

DAILY IN THE WORD
Ephesians 1:20-23

Paul described how the power of God has been made known through the Messiah. Through that power, God raised Jesus from the dead and seated Him at "His right hand in the heavens" (v. 20). Jesus Christ rules over every power, whether human or spiritual. He rules in this age, and He will rule in the age to come. Here, victory in spiritual warfare is assured on the basis of the One who fights for us.

The power of God was made evident in Jesus, but God didn't limit His power to the Messiah. As Christians, we have the power of God readily available to us. Christ is the head of all things for the benefit of the church, and we reap the blessings of sharing His power.

Christians have the power of God readily available.

APPLICATION
- Thank God that Christ rules over all things.
- Ask God for His power to overcome a particular sin in your life. Wear the breastplate of righteousness.

MEMORY VERSE FOR THIS WEEK
"I pray that the God of our Lord Jesus Christ, the glorious Father, would give you a spirit of wisdom and revelation in the knowledge of Him." Ephesians 1:17

day  *five*

TOUGH CHOICES IN THE GRAY AREAS

Imagine this scenario: Jim is committed to reaching his friends for Christ and has worked hard to develop strong relationships with them. He's let them know his standard of right and wrong, but aside from teasing him about it, they haven't made it an issue. They share a lot of hobbies and interests that are safe ground. Tonight one of his friends invited Jim to go with them to see a popular R-rated movie. Jim has made a commitment not to attend movies with overt sexual sin and gratuitous violence. However, he feels seeing this movie with his friends might lead to a conversation starter afterwards. This "gray area" confuses him.

What would you recommend that Jim do?

_____

What "gray areas" do you face?

- ❏ R-rated movies
- ❏ magazines that don't lead to godly thoughts
- ❏ TV shows that demean parents
- ❏ taking office supplies for personal use
- ❏ toying with sin in your mind
- ❏ a watercooler relationship with someone of the opposite sex

This lesson will provide guiding questions to help us make good decisions when we face such situations. We want to wear the breastplate of righteousness always.

Question 1—Do I Know Enough of the Bible to be Certain that It Doesn't Speak to This Topic?

This important question relates to the belt of truth, the breastplate of righteousness, and (as we shall see in later weeks) the sword of the Spirit. The Bible is our guide for living that is "profitable for teaching, for rebuking, for correcting, for training in righteousness, so that the man of God may be complete, equipped for every good work" (2 Tim. 3:16-17). We need to know it well in order to make decisions like the one Jim faced.

Sometimes we know just enough to be reckless in our decisions. Maybe you've heard these types of comments:

- "I've never read anything in the Bible about gambling, so it must not be wrong."
- "Well, Paul told Timothy to take some wine for his stomach, so God must allow some drinking now and then."
- "They didn't even have movies in the days of the Bible, so how can the Bible speak to this issue?"
- "I'm sure they had swear words in Bible days. God knows I don't mean it."

I trust that you get the point. Just because we haven't read anything in the Bible about a certain topic doesn't necessarily mean that the topic isn't addressed. Or, the fact that we remember a single Bible text doesn't show that we know the full extent of the Bible's teaching on that topic. For example, "I know divorce is not good, but look, Jesus forgave a woman who had been married *five* times. God wouldn't want me to stay in an unhappy marriage." But you can just as easily look at Matthew 19:9, which says, "Whoever divorces his wife, except for sexual immorality, and marries another, commits adultery." Many passages in the Bible deal with divorce, and you need to consider all of them to make a biblically-based decision. Start with Genesis 2:24. You can use a Bible concordance to find many passages that contain the word *divorce*.

Be honest about your familiarity with the Bible. If you don't know the Bible well enough to make a biblically-informed decision about your issue, get guidance from someone who does. Again, remember that we put on the armor of God with the help of other believers.

Put an "x" at the point on the following scale that describes your knowledge of the Bible at this point in your Christian journey.

1	2	3	4	5
very little knowledge	some knowledge		growing knowledge	significant knowledge

Question 2—What Biblical Principles Might Guide Me?

Sometimes life would be easier if every issue we faced were addressed in the Ten Commandments (though they would then become something like the Million Commandments). If *everything* wrong were preceded by the phrase "Thou shalt not," at least the gray areas would be clear. But God hasn't always given us such indisputable direction.

Sometimes God gives us principles to guide us, and we must learn to apply these biblical teachings when needed. The following principles should help you when you are faced with gray areas.

My actions should not be a stumbling block to others. To understand this principle, read 1 Corinthians 8:1-13. Paul addressed the issue of whether Christians should eat meat that had been offered to idols. This issue was especially important, as it was customary in the first century to offer meat to idols prior to selling or serving it. His answer followed this line of argument:

1. An idol really is nothing, as there is only one true God (vv. 4-6). By implication, eating meat offered to idols isn't inherently wrong.
2. What we eat or don't eat will not commend us to God, *but* some believers don't yet understand that meat offered to idols is nothing. Their conscience still views eating meat offered to idols as wrong (vv. 7-8).
3. If the actions of a stronger believer (who understands that meat offered to idols is nothing) lead a weaker believer to do what he thinks is wrong (eating that same meat), the stronger believer has sinned. He has allowed his Christian liberty to wound the conscience of a weaker brother (vv. 9-13).

The principle is that if my actions (even those I believe aren't wrong) cause another believer to sin, I have wrongfully become a stumbling block to that person. The believer wearing the breastplate of righteousness should refuse to cause a brother to stumble (v. 13).

Counter this argument: If someone else is tempted by something I do, that's really their problem, and they need to get over it.

_____

_____

My actions should build up others. Now read 1 Corinthians 10:23-30, a passage that addresses similar issues. Here, Paul recognized Christian freedom to purchase meat in the first-century market without asking whether the meat had been offered to idols; after all, everything ultimately belongs to the Lord (vv. 25-26). Likewise, believers may eat meat in the home of a nonbeliever, again without asking questions about idol worship (v. 27). If, however, the nonbeliever announces that the meat has been offered to idols, believers are wise not to eat the meat—lest another be offended (vv. 28-29). While Paul recognizes his freedom to eat or not to eat (vv. 29-30), his freedom ends when it leads another astray.

"Whether you eat or drink, or whatever you do, do everything for God's glory." *1 Corinthians 10:31*

More specifically, his freedom ends if his actions don't build up (edify) others. If he chooses to act in ways that are lawful to him but not edifying to someone else, he has not chosen the wise path. Wearing the breastplate of righteousness means choosing to put others before ourselves—even when our choices in the gray areas seem right to us.

My actions must glorify God. Ultimately, we are to do *whatever we do* so that we please and glorify God. Glorifying God means denying self and focusing on Him. It means being willing to sacrifice your desires on behalf of others (which sounds like Christ, doesn't it?).

For Paul, honoring God meant his willingness to give up much—even though he believed his Christian freedom didn't always require him to do so—for "the profit of many, that they may be saved" (1 Cor. 10:33). Wearing the breastplate of righteousness is as much about others as it is about us. As a child, I saw the anguish caused by excessive use of alcohol. As a pastor, I often ministered in homes torn apart by alcohol abuse. Given my history, combined with the principles previously listed, I believe *any* alcohol use for me is wrong.

I believe that the same arguments call all believers to abstinence. What is your response? Write your thoughts in the margin.

A Review: Wearing the Full Armor of God

Wearing the breastplate of righteousness means that we live as Jesus did: to please the Father and let nothing get in the way of this goal. Do you see how closely this piece of armor is related to the belt of truth? Living righteously as Jesus did requires that we know Him personally, know His Word, and live His Word. The breastplate of righteousness can't be separated from the belt of truth. The interconnected nature of the pieces of armor will be evident throughout this study and will help us understand why Paul said we must wear all of the armor of God. Only when we wear all of God's armor are we equipped and deployed for spiritual warfare.

DAILY IN THE WORD
Ephesians 2:1-3

Paul continued the theological portion by using four descriptions of the former life of believers. First, we were "dead" in our "trespasses and sins" (v. 1). We were on the path to eternal death. Second, we "walked according to this worldly age" as we followed the morals of a world in opposition to God (v. 2). Third, we "walked according ... to the ruler of the atmospheric domain"—the Devil (v. 2). Fourth, we lived according to the flesh, our sinful nature that seeks satisfaction apart from God. All of us, Paul said, live according to our flesh and will receive God's wrath. The story would be bleak if it ended here.

APPLICATION
- Think about your life before Christ. Thank God for His willingness to change you.
- Focus on what would have happened to you had God not called you to Him in salvation.

MEMORY VERSE FOR THIS WEEK
"I pray that the God of our Lord Jesus Christ, the glorious Father, would give you a spirit of wisdom and revelation in the knowledge of Him." Ephesians 1:17

1. The content of this lesson is used by permission from John Franklin and Chuck Lawless, *Spiritual Warfare: Biblical Truth for Victory* (Nashville: LifeWay, 2001), 55-58.
2. Robert D. Bergen, "1, 2 Samuel," in *New American Commentary* (Nashville: Broadman & Holman, 1996), 364.

Case Study

Your pastor has come to speak to your group. He is concerned about two major issues in your church. First, he believes the members really don't know the Bible very well. Second, he's burdened that too many members are living unrighteously. "They attend regularly," he says, "but I hear they live like the world the rest of the week."

Now, he wants your group to help him plan some strategies to address these issues. Knowing the topic of your study, he says to you, "I guess I want you to help me lead the church to wear the belt of truth and the breastplate of righteousness."

List some practical steps that your church could do to help members wear these two pieces of armor. Be as specific as possible, and be prepared to discuss your ideas with your group. Your pastor may want to see your group's list.

KNOWING THE BIBLE	LIVING MORE RIGHTEOUSLY

Feet Sandaled with the Gospel of Peace

Ann Miller has developed a close friendship with Brianne, a neighbor who also has children of high school and college age. They often have lunch just to talk about the stresses of relating to young adult children. Brianne is a great friend, but she isn't a Christian.

Recently, Ann has felt a strong urge to share her faith with her neighbor. Sure, she's invited Brianne to church, but she has never asked her specifically about her personal relationship with Christ. Twice now, Ann has begun the conversation and then retreated. "There's so much at risk," she thinks. "What if she doesn't listen to me? And what if she doesn't want to be my friend anymore? I couldn't take that—I need her friendship in my life so much right now."

At the same time, Ann has no peace about her decision. Might the Enemy have discouraged Ann from talking to her neighbor about her faith? What will it take for Ann to have inner peace about this situation? Could it be that she's not wearing part of the armor: "and [have] your feet sandaled with readiness for the gospel of peace" (Eph. 6:15)?

Although sandaled feet don't sound like weapons of war, Paul put this piece of the armor right in the middle of the other pieces. In day 1 I'll explain why and how to wear the sandaled feet of the armor. Days 2 and 3 address our peace with God and others. The final two days remind us of our responsibility to tell others about the gospel of peace.

REVIEWING THE FULL ARMOR OF GOD

Belt of _____
- Know Jesus.
- Know His Word.
- Live the Word.

Breastplate of _____
- Live like Jesus.
- Make right choices.
- Resist temptation.

day *one*

STANDING READY FOR THE BATTLE

You've probably seen the picture that marks the celebration of Japanese surrender in World War II—you know, the picture of the American sailor kissing a young nurse in the middle of New York City. The passion of that kiss symbolized the excitement of a nation for whom a long war was coming to an end. *Peace* was on the horizon. The peace that God has given us already is available today. In this peace we stand ready for spiritual battles that we might face.

Sandaled with Readiness?

Several versions of the Bible offer slightly different expressions of the same text in Ephesians 6:15:

"having shod your feet with the preparation of the gospel of peace" (NASB)

"with your feet fitted with the readiness that comes from the gospel of peace" (NIV)

"our feet sandaled with readiness for the gospel of peace" (HCSB)

"having shod your feet with the equipment of the gospel of peace" (RSV)

The differences revolve around the word translated variously as "preparation," "readiness," or "equipment." The term speaks of preparedness, and we best understand it as being ready for the battle. The question is, are we ready for the battle?

**How ready are you for spiritual battles that you face daily?
On a scale of 1-10, rate your personal readiness.**

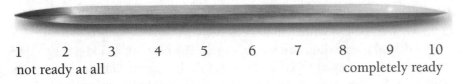

1	2	3	4	5	6	7	8	9	10

not ready at all   completely ready

From my experience, most believers aren't ready for spiritual battles. Putting on the armor is about learning to walk as Christ requires, but many churches don't teach believers how to do that. They reach new believers, baptize them, and fail to mentor them beyond that point. The Enemy doesn't back off just because believers are discipled, though, and too often he wins the battle. Take some time to thank God that your church has encouraged you to study this course that focuses on discipleship. After your group is finished with this study, God may use you to help another believer because you'll be prepared.

If the first question is "Are we ready for the battle?" a following question is "How do we get ready for the battle?" On one hand, we are at peace with God. On the other hand, we are at war with the Enemy. As we shall see, getting ready for the battle involves both defensive and offensive actions.

Getting Ready: "Standing" on the Defensive

Some scholars have understood that the footwear imagery of this piece of the armor reflects the armament of a Roman soldier, who often wore boots equipped with long nails for solid footing. The image shows that we should anchor down against the Enemy's attacks. In fact, the word translated "stand" in Ephesians 6:13 is a military term meaning "take your position and hold it." We defend our ground simply by standing firmly.

> **Clearly, one aspect of our response to spiritual attack is defensive. Read the Scriptures below and underline the believer's responses that seem to be more defensive than offensive.**

Be alert, stand firm in the faith, be brave and strong (1 Cor. 16:13).

Submit to God. But resist the Devil, and he will flee from you (Jas. 4:7).

Be sober! Be on the alert! Your adversary the Devil is prowling around like a roaring lion, looking for anyone he can devour. Resist him, firm in the faith (1 Pet. 5:8-9).

As believers, we are to be watchful and alert, always aware of the spiritual forces around us. We submit to God, trusting Him to give us the power to resist the Devil. He may try to terrify us with his roar, but we are to stand against him with our faith.

I'm a fan of white-water rafting and have been on several trips. Just before we hit a rapid, the guide hollers, "Lock in! Lock in!"—which means to stabilize your feet to prevent being tossed from the raft. That's one way to understand Paul's command to stand ready against the Enemy. It's as if he says, "Lock in, lock in!" and be ready for the battle.

How do we stand ready to defend against the Enemy? Let's focus on five of the many ways to defend yourself.

1. **Resist temptation when the Enemy seeks to lead you into sin.** The principles we learned last week will help us here.
2. **Stay faithful even when the battle rages.** The peace that God gives us does not necessarily mean an absence of conflict. In fact, sometimes "peace" means having a heart that remains comforted and faithful during, and in spite of, a conflict. God gives us a calm that the world can't understand, and we resist the Devil when we stand in that peace (Phil. 4:6-7).
3. **Refuse to compromise biblical truth.** From the events of Genesis 3 until today, the Enemy has encouraged people to doubt or deny God's Word. We stand against this strategy when we learn, affirm, and teach biblical truth.
4. **Keep your eyes on God in spite of distractions.** The Enemy loves to catch our attention, turning our eyes from God toward the problems we face. We prepare ahead of time by deciding we won't allow our circumstances to overshadow our focus on Him.
5. **March forward in faith at any given moment.** When God calls us to take a step of faith, the prepared spiritual warrior moves without hesitation. He is equipped and always ready to be deployed.

The peace that God gives us does not necessarily mean an absence of conflict.

We are ready for the battle when we are prepared to fight temptation, to remain steadfast, to stand for truth, to keep our eyes on God, and to march at God's command. How locked in are you for the battle?

Ask God to reveal to you your defensive status. For each of the five defensive positions, indicate your level of readiness on a scale of 1 to 5 with 1 being "not at all ready" and 5 being "very ready."

____ ready to resist temptation

____ ready to stay faithful even when the battle seems to be going the wrong way

____ ready to refuse to compromise biblical truth

____ ready to keep my eyes on God

____ ready to march forward in faith

Getting Ready: Moving Out on the Offensive

The language of Ephesians 6:15 sounds remarkably like Isaiah 52:7 in the margin. In that verse, a messenger proclaims peace, good news, and salvation—and Isaiah says the messenger's feet are beautiful. The connection between these verses implies that having our feet sandaled isn't only defensive but also offensive: sharing the gospel.

We should always be ready to share the good news of Christ. We are to teach the Word, persisting "in it whether convenient or not" (2 Tim. 4:2), always being ready to give a defense for our faith (1 Pet. 3:15). When we are always prepared to tell somebody about Jesus, we stand against the Enemy.

One of my heroes in the faith was known as "Brother Jack." As a young preacher, Brother Jack indicated on his seminary application that he wanted to spend the rest of his life telling people about Jesus. For the next 60 years, he served in ministry and shared the gospel wherever he went. When I was with him in a public setting, I knew he wouldn't miss an opportunity to tell somebody else about Jesus. I pray I will have that boldness, always being ready to proclaim the gospel to others.

This offensive aspect of standing ready is so important. The following activity will help you to see how ready you are to tell others about Jesus.

Mark each statement as true *(T)*, false *(F)*, or uncertain *(U)* to reflect your personal readiness to do evangelism.

____ I look for opportunities to tell others the good news of Jesus.

____ I don't look for opportunities to evangelize.

____ I probably miss some opportunities to evangelize.

____ It's been a long time since I told someone about Christ.

____ I will pray for opportunities to speak about Jesus this week.

> "How beautiful on the mountains
> are the feet of the herald,
> who proclaims peace,
> who brings news of good things,
> who proclaims salvation,
> who says to Zion, 'Your God reigns!'" *Isaiah 52:7*

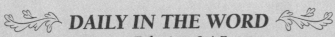

DAILY IN THE WORD
Ephesians 2:4-7

In week 2 we read Ephesians 2:1-3, which spoke about the fact that we were "under wrath" because of our sin. In verse 4 Paul made a sudden shift to the doctrines of mercy, love, and grace. This shift is set off by the simple but powerful phrase "but God." God in His abundant mercy and great love treats us with favor even though we are undeserving (v. 4). In the past we were dead, but He gives us life here and in the resurrection. We had been children under wrath, but now He gives us the privilege of being "seated … with Him in the heavens" (v. 6). We followed the Enemy, but now we are—and will forever be—a display of God's grace and kindness.

The focus here is God, who rescued us from our past ways. Keeping that focus will help us when we face spiritual battles.

APPLICATION
- Make a list of God's blessings in the margin. Throughout the day, think about God's goodness.
- Thank God for His grace to you.

MEMORY VERSE FOR THIS WEEK
"By grace you are saved through faith, and this is not from yourselves; it is God's gift—not from works, so that no one can boast."
Ephesians 2:8-9

day *two*

OUR RELATIONSHIP WITH GOD

As I write this lesson, the United States and Iraq are at war. We know that the costs of any war are typically high. In this case, American and Iraqi families have been forever changed by the loss of a spouse, parent, son, or daughter. Billions of dollars have been spent. Peace, when it comes, will not have come without a cost. In day 2 I will emphasize another kind of peace—the peace God gives us when we are His children. That peace cost God His Son. When we better understand this gospel of peace, we should be more willing to stand against the Enemy's wiles.

Apart from Christ, We Are at War with God

This heading might sound odd, as this study concerns warfare with the Devil rather than with God. Yet, the Bible teaches us that we are at odds with God apart from redemption in Christ. That truth is even more fundamental than the truth that believers battle with the Enemy. Without salvation, we remain in the "domain of darkness" (Col. 1:13).

Read Ephesians 2:1-3 in the margin. List the words or phrases that describe our lives prior to meeting Jesus.

_____

_____

"You were dead in your trespasses and sins in which you previously walked according to this worldly age, according to the ruler of the atmospheric domain, the spirit now working in the disobedient. We too all previously lived among them in our fleshly desires, carrying out the inclinations of our flesh and thoughts, and by nature we were children under wrath, as the others were also."
Ephesians 2:1-3

You probably found words like "dead in trespasses and sins," "sons of disobedience," and "children of wrath." Listen to other phrases that describe our desperate situation:

- "All have turned away; all alike have become corrupt. There is no one who does good, not even one" (Ps. 14:3).
- "The wicked go astray from the womb; liars err from birth" (Ps. 58:3).
- "All our righteous acts are like a polluted garment" (Isa. 64:6).
- "Those whose lives are in the flesh are unable to please God" (Rom. 8:8).
- "To those who are defiled and unbelieving nothing is pure; in fact, both their mind and conscience are defiled" (Titus 1:15).

Do you hear any sense of hope in these statements? There's none, as all of us are without hope apart from Christ. In fact, perhaps the heading of this section is too strong, as it implies that we are somehow strong enough to battle against God. If we are indeed at war with God, we have already lost the war and have no hope of winning a single battle.

There Is No Gospel of Peace Apart from Jesus

If our story ended with the previous paragraph, we would obviously be in a deep depression. But here's the good news. Through His death, Jesus reconciled us to the Father. In the latter section of Ephesians 2, Paul explained that Christ united Gentiles and Jews alike under His grace.

> **Read more of Ephesians 2 listed below, and circle the word *peace* each time you see it.**

> He is our peace, who made both groups one and tore down the dividing wall of hostility. In His flesh, He did away with the law of the commandments in regulations, so that He might create in Himself one new man from the two, resulting in peace. When Christ came, He proclaimed the good news of peace to you who were far away and peace to those who were near (2:14-15,17).

Jesus is the "Prince of Peace" (Isa. 9:6) whose sacrificial death bridges the gap between us and God. We can be at peace with God not because we deserve it, but because Jesus is our mediator (1 Tim. 2:5). He became sin for us (2 Cor. 5:21), bore God's wrath against us (Rom. 3:23-26), and now advocates for us with the Father (1 John 2:1). That which put us at odds with God—our sinfulness—has now been addressed.

Every year I remember the day that God saved me in August of 1974. Even though I was young, I had heard just enough of the gospel that I feared death. Sleep was difficult, as I worried each night what might happen to me if I were to die during the night. When God saved me, though, I slept like a baby for the first time in many months. No peace exists like the peace God gives us when our relationship with Him is restored. Jesus *is* that peace, and He makes that peace possible.

No peace exists like the peace God gives us when our relationship with Him is restored.

Check any of the following statements that reflect your thinking.

❑ I haven't thought very much about how Jesus' death gives me peace with God.
❑ I'm not sure what it means to be at peace with God.
❑ I've taken for granted that Jesus died to give me peace with God.
❑ I genuinely appreciate Jesus as the source of my peace with God.

Peace with God Is Not Only Positional but Also Practical

We learned in week 1 that as Christians, our position is "in Christ" (Eph. 1:1,4,7, 12-13). That is, He is the one who chooses us, saves us, seals us, and keeps us. We are Christians because of what He has done rather than because of what we've done.

We aren't saying that how we live doesn't matter. In fact, Paul urged believers to "walk worthy of the calling you have received" (Eph. 4:1). Because we are positionally "in Christ," we demonstrate that position practically by living righteously. Christ in us should be evidenced in our Christian words and actions. Since I've stressed this truth throughout the study, it shouldn't be new to you!

Simon Peter was one of the three disciples with whom Jesus spent the most time. His story helps us understand the link between our actions and experiencing God's peace. Read his story in Luke 22:54-60.

What do you think Peter felt as he three times denied the One he loved?

_____

Do you believe he was comfortable with his actions? ❑ yes ❑ no
Do you think he felt peace? ❑ yes ❑ no

> "The Lord turned and looked at Peter. So Peter remembered the word of the Lord, how He had said to him, 'Before the rooster crows today, you will deny Me three times.' And he went outside and wept bitterly." *Luke 22:61-62*

Clearly, Peter made his own wrong choice, but his impassioned denials suggest that he was battling within himself even as he sinned. We also know that he "wept bitterly" when he was forced to face his wrongdoing (see Luke 22:61-62 in margin). Surely these tears were evidence of great internal turmoil.

When we sin, that's what happens to us as well. Guilt and conviction quickly replace the temporary pleasure of sin, and we are rightly robbed of our inner peace. Only genuine confession and repentance followed by God's forgiveness will restore that peace (1 John 1:9).

Place an "x" on the following scale at the place that best indicates your "practical" peace with God.

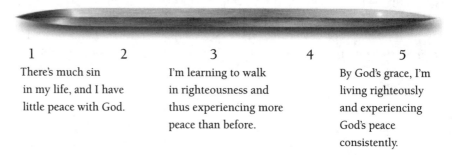

1	2	3	4	5
There's much sin in my life, and I have little peace with God.		I'm learning to walk in righteousness and thus experiencing more peace than before.		By God's grace, I'm living righteously and experiencing God's peace consistently.

Our Peace with God Is Unexplainable

In another letter Paul wrote from prison, the apostle said this "peace of God, which surpasses every thought, will guard your hearts and your minds in Christ Jesus" (Phil. 4:7). Human minds can't comprehend the peace that God gives us, because His peace isn't circumstantial. The battles can rage around us, and still we can have an unexplainable peace on the inside. The world doesn't understand that kind of peace; this peace can come only from God.

In one church where I served as pastor, a lady known as Mrs. Lucy modeled that kind of peace. She outlived her husband and a son, and she endured the imprisonment of a grandson. Still, she never complained, and her faith never wavered. Mrs. Lucy died trusting that Christ awaited her. Even the Enemy cannot disrupt the peace that God gives. If you know someone who has modeled that kind of peace for you, write that name in the margin. Ask God to help you stand against the Enemy with His peace.

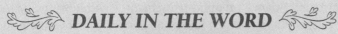

DAILY IN THE WORD
Ephesians 2:8-10

Today's reading covers some of the best known verses in Ephesians, but it also includes one of the most overlooked. As Paul continued, he laid out God's plan by which we are saved. First, "by grace you are saved" (v. 8). Paul used the identical wording at the end of verse 5. Teachers use repetition as a common tool for emphasis, so he must have wanted us to catch this truth. We are saved by nothing we do. Only what God graciously does within us brings salvation.

Second, this grace is available only "through faith" (v. 8). Faith relies on and believes in a trustworthy God. Finally (in the passage often overlooked), we are "created in Christ Jesus for good works" (v. 10). Good works are not the means of salvation but the assumed by-product of it.

APPLICATION
- Decide to trust God in faith throughout this day. If you face a difficult time, trust Him anyway.
- Do some good deeds or works today—simply because God saved you to do so.

MEMORY VERSE FOR THIS WEEK
"By grace you are saved through faith, and this is not from yourselves; it is God's gift—not from works, so that no one can boast."
Ephesians 2:8-9

Good works are not the means of salvation but the assumed by-product of it.

day *three*

OUR RELATIONSHIP WITH OTHERS

I teach several spiritual warfare conferences each year. During most conferences, I ask participants to think about the events in the garden of Eden in Genesis 3. We discuss our Enemy's methods and strategies, and we examine the responses of Adam and Eve. Specifically, we focus on Adam and Eve, who hid themselves from God after they sinned.

"God confronted Adam," I remind participants, "and how did Adam respond?" Almost without exception, the men know the answer and are willing shout it: "This woman is the problem! *She* led me astray."

What usually brings a chuckle from the crowd is really the reflection of a fundamental truth about spiritual warfare: the Enemy aims his arrows at relationships. In the first four chapters of Genesis, he successfully fosters division and strife in the first family. The Enemy simply doesn't want us to have peace with one another.

This study stresses our responsibility to be at peace with others, based on our relationship with God. Only when we are first at peace with Him can we be at peace with others.

Relationships Matter

Read the following Scriptures, and briefly describe what each says about relationships.

1. Exodus 20:12 _____

_____

2. Deuteronomy 6:4 _____

_____

3. Ephesians 4:1 _____

_____

4. Ephesians 5:22 _____

_____

5. 1 Peter 3:7 _____

_____

We are to honor our parents. Parents should teach their children the truths of the Bible. Believers must accept one another in love. Husbands are expected to love their wives as Christ loves the church. In fact, their prayers are hindered if they don't treat their wives appropriately. Relationships clearly matter. Why are relationships so important? If we understand this truth, we will also know why the Enemy so often strikes at relationships.

First, healthy relationships reflect the nature of God. Solid Christian marriages teach love that is sacrificial, giving, and unashamed. Good Christian parenting shows unconditional love that includes nurturing discipline. Godly friendships show affirming, supportive, and even confrontational love. In each case, we learn more about the nature of God as experienced in the context of relationships.

Second, healthy relationships are a witness to others. If a Christian husband loves his wife properly, others ought to see in that relationship how Christ loves the church. Unbelievers ought to see in a Christian home something different from what they experience in their own homes. In the end, perhaps they will seek the One who is the cornerstone of Christian relationships and homes. Relationships that point others to Jesus really do matter.

Unity Matters

John 17 records a lengthy prayer that Jesus prayed not long before His betrayal in the garden of Gethsemane. Read the following verses and underline any phrases that speak of unity.

I pray not only for these, but also for those who believe in Me through their message. May they all be one, as You, Father, are in Me and I am in You. May they also be one in Us, so the world may believe You sent Me. I have given them the glory You have given Me. May they be one as We are one. I am in them and You are in Me. May they be made completely one, so the world may know You have sent Me and have loved them as You have loved Me (John 17:20-23).

Jesus prayed that the relationships of believers would be just as united as His own relationship with the Father. Indeed, four times in these verses He called for such unity—because He understood that unity would be a witness to the world.

Think about it. One local church may have members from different economic, educational, and social backgrounds. More than one ethnic group may be represented. Some may prefer hymns, and others like praise choruses. Not everyone uses the same version of the Bible. Somehow, though, the church marches forward under a common vision to fulfill the Great Commission (Matt. 28:18-20). How does that happen when such diversity exists in the church body?

In West Africa, where most of the believers don't speak English, their worship style is lively and their services are much longer than ours. Still, I had the privilege and ability to worship with our African brothers and sisters despite these barriers. How does that happen?

The answer in both cases is simple: God unites His church. When a broken, messed-up world sees that oneness—that is, that we love each other in spite of differences and can unite around a common mission—they see a miracle. Only God can make such things happen. (The unity I speak of here is a unity built solidly upon biblical truth. Unity that comes at the compromise of biblical truth is not godly unity at all.) Conversely, when the world sees believers who quarrel and bicker, they have little interest in being a part of God's church.

Evaluate your church's unity. Use the second scale to evaluate whether your contribution is to unity or disunity.

My church is …

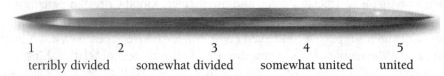

1	2	3	4	5
terribly divided	somewhat divided	somewhat united		united

My contribution …

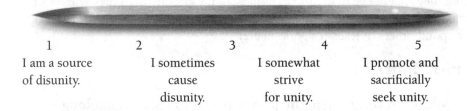

1	2	3	4	5
I am a source of disunity.	I sometimes cause disunity.	I somewhat strive for unity.		I promote and sacrificially seek unity.

STEPS TO FORGIVING OTHERS

1. Admit my anger and ask God's forgiveness.
2. Ask God to help me to let go of my pain.
3. Meditate on God's grace toward me.
4. Pray for the other person.
5. Focus on doing good toward others. The change of focus away from my anger will be liberating.

Forgiveness Matters

Because unity matters, so does forgiving one another. Read Jesus' words below. Spend time contemplating them. If you are challenged by His words, ask God for grace to hear and follow them.

If you are offering your gift on the altar, and there you remember that your brother has something against you, leave your gift there in front of the altar. First go and be reconciled with your brother, and then come and offer your gift (Matt. 5:23-24).

If you forgive people their wrongdoing, your heavenly Father will forgive you as well. But if you don't forgive people, your Father will not forgive your wrongdoing (Matt. 6:14-15).

These words are indeed difficult. Jesus teaches us that our peace with God relates directly to our peace with others, and He doesn't allow us room to be bitter and unforgiving. In fact, He calls us to take the initiative toward reconciliation even when we are not necessarily the offending party.

Why is forgiving others so important? We model God's forgiving love when we forgive others (see Matt. 18:21-35). In an unforgiving world, God's love bears a unique witness. Moreover, God demands obedience, and not forgiving is disobedience. He commands us to forgive others even when we don't feel like it or when the guilty party doesn't ask for forgiveness.

Forgiving others also frees us from the bondage of our pain. While we may not forget the pain, it no longer controls us. Finally, forgiving others closes a door through which the Enemy seeks to enter our lives. He continually searches for entrances, and an unforgiving heart leaves a wide-open door.

Are you at peace with others? Do you need to forgive someone?

Indicate that you agree (*A*), disagree (*D*), or are uncertain (*U*).

_____ 1. There's no one I need to forgive.
_____ 2. I know I need to forgive someone, but I'm not ready yet.
_____ 3. I am trying hard to forgive someone, but I'm struggling.
_____ 4. God graciously helped me to forgive someone who hurt me.
_____ 5. Bitterness and anger are controlling my life.

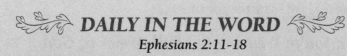

DAILY IN THE WORD
Ephesians 2:11-18

Throughout the Bible we are told to remember. For example, we are to remember the Sabbath (Ex. 20:8), our Creator (Eccl. 12:1), and Jesus' death (1 Cor. 11:23-25). In today's Bible reading, Paul instructed his readers to remember the time when they didn't know the Messiah. The Gentiles Paul addressed in this section were once without the Messiah, apart from God, and without hope.

Christ, though, was their peace who brings believers—both Jew and Gentile—together. No longer could any regulations and laws exclude the Gentiles from becoming believers. Instead, Jesus preached a gospel of peace that tore down hostilities and created one body that was neither Jew nor Gentile: the Church.

APPLICATION
- Remember today what God did in your life to draw you to Him.
- Reach out today to someone unlike you—someone who might need to know the gospel of peace.

MEMORY VERSE FOR THIS WEEK
"By grace you are saved through faith, and this is not from yourselves; it is God's gift—not from works, so that no one can boast."
Ephesians 2:8-9

day *four*

GETTING READY
TO TELL THE STORY

I met Tony on a plane. Tony saw me reading my Bible, and he quickly began telling me about how he had recently met Christ. Two hours later, he was still talking about how Jesus had changed his life! All I did was listen, and I left that plane wanting to tell everybody about Jesus.

How can we not tell others this story? All of us were separated from God by our sin (Rom. 3:23), with death as the judgment for this sin (Rom. 6:23). Yet Christ died for us while we were still sinners (Rom. 5:6-8). Through God's grace, we can have peace with Him. Christ died for us, and we can be restored to a right relationship with God (and ultimately, with others). What awesome news!

Remember from day 1 that believers who are prepared for the battle are those who stand ready to proclaim the gospel. Day 4 will help us understand the relationship between evangelism and spiritual warfare. Then we will identify the first steps toward getting ready to share the gospel.

Make Sure You're Wearing the Full Armor of God

This step in the process shouldn't be a surprise to you. Wearing the full armor of God is essential to faithful Christian living and not just to witnessing. We trust that you're studying this topic because you want to wear the armor *and* be the most effective witness that you can be.

At this point we have looked at only the first three pieces of the armor. To be a strong witness for Christ, you will want to evaluate your own life week by week through the rest of the study. For now, think about how these three pieces of the armor have impacted you.

Write specific steps you have taken over the last few weeks to wear each piece of this armor.

belt of truth _____

_____

breastplate of righteousness _____

_____

feet sandaled _____

_____

Understand that Unbelievers Are Blinded by the Enemy

A second step toward evangelizing the unsaved is to make certain our theology about lost persons is correct. Read 2 Corinthians 4:3-4 in the margin, and answer these questions:

1. What is the state of unbelievers? _____

2. Who has created this blindness? _____

"If in fact, our gospel is veiled, it is veiled to those who are perishing. Regarding them: the god of this age has blinded the minds of the unbelievers so they cannot see the light of the gospel of the glory of Christ, who is the image of God." 2 Corinthians 4:3-4

The Apostle Paul was committed to telling others about the good news of Christ. In fact, he knew that God had called him to do just that. God would use him to "open their eyes that they may turn from darkness to light and from the power of Satan to God, that they may receive forgiveness of sins" (Acts 26:18).

Paul also understood, though, that he couldn't change people in his own ability, for "the god of this age has blinded the minds of the unbelievers" (2 Cor. 4:4). "The god of this age" is a reference to Satan, who is also called the "ruler of this world" (John 16:11) and the "ruler of the atmospheric domain" (Eph. 2:2). Paul knew that no human power could change the minds the Enemy had blinded.

We find this truth hard to swallow if we have friends and loved ones who are nonbelievers. I have family members who aren't Christians, and this teaching is painful. However, the truth of the Scriptures always trumps our emotions. One step in getting ready to share the gospel is simply accepting and believing the truth that persons who don't know Jesus personally are lost.

In the margin, list the names of two persons you believe are blinded by the Enemy. Ask God to open their minds to His truth.

Get Others to Pray for You

When Paul concluded the list of armor in Ephesians 6, he then asked the believers to pray for him. His request was simple but significant.

Read Ephesians 6:19-20 in the margin. Write Paul's specific prayer in your own words:

_____

_____

> "Pray also for me, that the message may be given to me when I open my mouth to make known with boldness the mystery of the gospel. For this I am an ambassador in chains. Pray that I might be bold enough in Him to speak as I should." *Ephesians 6:19-20*

Paul asked the believers to pray that he would "make known with boldness" the good news of Jesus. Why did Paul feel the need to ask for this kind of prayer support? He understood that evangelism is spiritual warfare—taking the gospel of light into the kingdom of darkness. If we're going to tell nonbelievers the good news of Jesus, we'd better be ready for the Enemy to fight against us.

The Evil One doesn't give up his captives easily, although he's no match for God's grace. At the same time, he aims his arrows at believers so that they won't be good witnesses. If he can disarm the believer, he temporarily wins the battle.

Think about how Satan disarms us. Sometimes fear of rejection shuts us down. At other times, we convince ourselves that our loved ones and friends are "good enough" for God to accept them. Or, maybe we think this way: "I'm not good enough to be a witness for God. He would never use me." Sometimes our sin is, in fact, so obvious that we lack credibility in our witness. In any of these cases, the Enemy wins when we choose not to engage in evangelism.

Paul certainly understood the Enemy's attacks, as he was imprisoned for preaching the gospel (Eph. 6:20). He didn't give up, though. Rather, he asked believers to pray for him so that he wouldn't miss a single opportunity to tell about Jesus. Paul knew that he not only couldn't open blinded minds but also he couldn't even evangelize in his own power. He needed the prayer support of other believers to speak boldly as the Enemy tried to disarm him.

If Paul needed the prayer support of armed prayer warriors, surely we do, too. Few of us have the boldness of the apostle. Ask God to give you the names of believers who will pray that you will be a bold witness. List their names here, and ask them this week to support you in prayer. The "GOD'S HEART" acrostic in the margin (p. 60) is one way for them to pray for you and for the nonbelievers you're trying to reach.

G=that believers will appreciate God's grace

O=that believers will be obedient

D=that believers will have a desire to tell others

S=that believers will speak the gospel fearlessly

H=for nonbelievers to have a receptive heart

E=that their spiritual eyes will be opened

A=that they will have God's attitude toward sin

R=that they will be released to believe

T=that their lives will be transformed[1]

My Potential Prayer Support Team

_____   _____

_____   _____

_____   _____

Ask God to Restore Your Fire for Evangelism

Have there been times for you when your fire for evangelism probably burned more strongly? For me, that time was when God first saved me. To be honest, I didn't worry at all about someone's rejection if I shared the gospel. Nor was I concerned that I wouldn't be prepared to answer all the questions someone might ask. All I knew was God had saved me, and I almost couldn't stop myself from proclaiming His goodness. Today I still evangelize, but I must admit that I often do so more out of obligation than out of the natural overflow of my walk with God.

Do you, too, remember days when you almost couldn't help but evangelize? ❑ yes ❑ no

If so, what do you think causes us to lose our fire?

_____

Here's one possibility: we get so busy doing good stuff at church that we get disconnected from a hurting and dying world. Others look at us and brag about our faithfulness at church. In the midst of all of that activity, though, we lose our burden for nonbelievers. Our *readiness* to share the gospel wanes.

Do you suppose the Enemy delights when good stuff distracts us from doing evangelism? While never denying the importance of good works, we must remember that evangelism is also a necessary good work. Only when we're ready and seeking to share the good news are our feet sandaled with the gospel of peace.

To be honest, even as I'm writing these words, I'm asking God to make my fire burn brightly again. Maybe that's why He let me meet Tony on that plane.

Ask God to reignite your fire for evangelism.

Dear God, _____

_____

_____

_____

_____

DAILY IN THE WORD
Ephesians 2:19-22

Today's reading continues the discussion about the peace Christ gives. The Gentiles are no longer "foreigners and strangers." Rather, they're welcomed into God's household (v. 19). They, along with the Jewish believers, serve the same Father and share the same Spirit. They stand on the same foundation and share the same cornerstone, Jesus Christ Himself. They're at peace with God and with one another.

The united believers constitute a new body, a "building" that is still under construction. They are, and are growing to be, holy people in whom God dwells. How different that picture is from the one in Ephesians 2:1-10! Those who were without the Messiah, and consequently without hope, were now growing as the very dwelling place of God. Only by the grace of God was this growth possible.

APPLICATION
- If you are not at peace with someone, seek reconciliation today.
- Meditate on this truth: God Himself lives in us through His Spirit.

MEMORY VERSE FOR THIS WEEK
"By grace you are saved through faith, and this is not from yourselves; it is God's gift—not from works, so that no one can boast."
Ephesians 2:8-9

> The united believers constitute a new body, a "building" that is still under construction.

day  five

TELLING THE STORY

In his book *The Art of Personal Evangelism*, Will McRaney Jr. writes, "Several experts suggest that 95 to 97 percent of American Christians do not share their faith with others."[2] While not presuming on God's sovereignty, think about the future of the church and of Christianity if that pattern continues. If a maximum of 5 percent of believers tell others about Jesus, how will we reach the millions of nonbelievers in this country? Who will reach the 1.6 billion people around the world who have no access to the gospel?

Obviously, God's church is His church, and He is ultimately responsible for its growth (Matt. 16:18). But He has called all of us to be His witnesses to the ends of the earth (Acts 1:8). Wearing the armor of God means that we are ready to tackle this challenge.

Day 4 laid the groundwork for sharing your faith. This lesson is designed to show you how to tell someone else about peace with Jesus—even if you have never done it before.

Be Prepared to Tell Your Story

Evangelism frightens and overwhelms many believers so they never witness. But evangelism is simply telling others what God has done in your life and then helping them know the good news of salvation. How did the Apostle Paul tell his story?

Read Acts 26:1-23 and answer the questions about Paul's life.

What was Paul's life like before he met Christ (vv. 1-11)? _____

_____

How did Paul learn that he needed to follow Christ (vv. 12-18)? _____

_____

_____

_____

How did Paul's life change when he met Christ (vv. 19-23)? _____

_____

_____

_____

Prior to his conversion, Paul was a Pharisee (a Jewish religious leader) who was zealous about his faith. He was so committed to Judaism that he punished and persecuted Christians. In fact, Paul was on his way to arrest other believers when God struck him down, confronted him, and called him to a new way of life. With the touch of God's grace, the persecutor became the preacher extraordinaire.

Telling your story is as simple as following Paul's pattern. Think about your own conversion. Describe the changes in your life then and now. Share the blessings of knowing you are eternally secure in the hands of God. Mention ways you are changing to be like Christ. Be prepared to tell this story to your group.

What was your life like before you met Christ? _____

_____

_____

How did you learn that you needed to follow Christ? _____

_____

_____

How did you make the decision to follow Christ? _____

_____

_____

How did your life change when you met Christ? _____

_____

_____

_____

Be Alert to Opportunities to Tell Others about Christ

Many times we struggle with learning how to move a conversation toward the gospel. A believer who stands ready for the battle, though, always watches for opportunities to share the gospel. Here are some simple steps to recognize those possibilities when they occur.

Intentionally develop relationships with nonbelievers. As a seminary professor who lives in the church world, I am surrounded most of the time by believers. One way I countered this problem was by joining a local gym rather than exercising in the seminary's recreation center. What options do you have to make sure you have relationships with unbelievers?

Know people—and always be prepared to minister to them when they're hurting. Recognizing that we should be careful not to manipulate people when they are in pain, we should still be ready to offer Christian help and love when needed. Any type of ministry such as preparing a meal, providing childcare, helping a shut-in with her lawn, visiting a hospitalized patient, or simply being a listening ear might pave the way to telling your story.

Do a prayer survey of those you encounter daily. Ask people such as your waiter at a restaurant, the person who throws your paper or drops off your mail, or neighbors you meet walking your dog or jogging if you can pray for them. For example, say, "I'm praying for my neighbors. Is there anything for which I might pray for you?" Some people may not verbalize a prayer need, but many will. Perhaps your question will open the door to talking more about your personal relationship with Christ.

Take the initiative to ask others about themselves. When you ask for information about others, they're likely to ask you more about yourself. Take advantage of that opportunity to tell them that you're a Christian and that Christ is the most important person in your life.

Be ready to respond appropriately when someone asks about your day or weekend. Most of us have someone ask us, "How are you doing today?" or "How was your weekend?" Our response is typically something superficial like "Fine" or "OK." Why not be prepared to answer with something like, "I'm having a great day because I'm a Christian and God loves me"?

Learn to bridge conversations to talk about your Christianity. Bridging is the process of moving a conversation in a direction that may give you an opportunity to speak about Christ. Ideally, we learn to take these steps naturally so our approach to evangelism isn't contrived or fake.

Jesus never missed an opportunity to speak the gospel. As we might expect, He was a master at bridging conversation to get there. He spoke of being "born again" to a Jew who assumed his physical birth made him God's child (John 3:1-21). He talked about "living water" to a woman at a well (John 4:1-29). He used the story of a sower to talk about the human heart (Matt. 13:1-9,18-23).

Think about ways to bridge a conversation to talk about Christianity so that you don't miss an opportunity. As you complete the following activity, maybe people who fit the characteristics described will come to mind. If so, you may want to say a quick prayer for them.

Draw a line from the situation on the left to the possible conversational bridge for sharing your faith on the right.

A conversation with …

1. a sports fanatic

2. a government official

3. a teacher

4. an atheist

5. an engineer

A. "God is very real to me. Help me understand why you think He doesn't exist."

B. "I pray for you every day, because the Bible tells us to pray for our leaders."

C. "Did you know that a writer in the Bible—Paul—talked a lot about sporting events?"

D. "Have you ever thought about how God designed and put the world together?"

E. "The greatest teacher I've ever known is Jesus."

Complete Your Church's Training to Share the Gospel

Telling our story or talking about Christianity is only a first step toward introducing others to Jesus. Ultimately, evangelism is telling the story of the good news:

• A holy God created us and holds us responsible for our actions.
• We have, by our nature and our actions, sinned against this Creator.
• God chose in grace and mercy to send His Son as an atonement for our wrong. Jesus took on Himself our sin, suffered the Father's judgment by dying for our sin, and was then resurrected.
• We are commanded to turn from our sin and believe in Jesus in response to God's drawing us to be His children. He gives us peace when we respond to Him.

If your church has an evangelism training program such as *FAITH* or *Share Jesus without Fear,* plan to complete that training when you finish this study. If your church has no evangelism training program, ask your pastor to begin one; or instead, ask someone you respect as a soul-winner to mentor you. We defeat the Enemy when we choose to be fully equipped and ready to proclaim the gospel of peace.

A Review: Wearing the Full Armor of God

Are you continuing to see why we must wear the *full* armor of God? Jesus is the Truth (John 14:6), our righteousness (2 Cor. 5:21), and our peace (Eph. 2:14). Knowing Him is essential to wearing the belt of truth, wearing the breastplate of righteousness, and experiencing the gospel of peace.

At the same time, we experience God's peace when we live truthfully and righteously—including telling others about Him. Wearing the full armor of God equips us for the battle, and God then deploys us to tell others about the gospel of peace.

DAILY IN THE WORD
Ephesians 3:1-7

In today's reading, Paul spoke about his ministry to the Gentiles. He was a "prisoner of Jesus Christ on behalf of the Gentiles" (v. 1). As a slave to Jesus, he had proclaimed the gospel to Jew and Gentile alike. This inclusive message was offensive to the Jews who had imprisoned Paul for his ministry to the Gentiles (Acts 21–22).

Paul saw himself as a servant of the gospel who was given the responsibility to speak this truth: Gentiles, too, were "co-heirs, members of the same body, and partners of the promise in Christ Jesus" (v. 6). He had received God's grace, and he must now speak about that grace to all others. Paul's ministry to the Gentiles ultimately laid the foundation for Christian missions as we know it today.

APPLICATION
- Thank God that Gentiles, too, are members of His church.
- Because you are a steward of God's grace, tell someone about His grace this week.

MEMORY VERSE FOR THIS WEEK
"By grace you are saved through faith, and this is not from yourselves; it is God's gift—not from works, so that no one can boast."
Ephesians 2:8-9

Answers to activity on page 64: 1. C; 2. B; 3. E; 4. A; 5. D

1. Charles E. Lawless Jr., *Serving in Your Church Prayer Ministry* (Grand Rapids: Zondervan, 2003), 71. See also "Praying Your Friends to Christ," [online], [cited 7 August 2006]. Available from Internet: *www.namb.net.*
2. Will McRaney Jr., *The Art of Personal Evangelism* (Nashville: Broadman & Holman, 2003), 5.

The Shield of Faith

REVIEWING THE FULL ARMOR OF GOD

Belt of _____
- Know Jesus.
- Know His Word.
- Live the Word.

Breastplate of _____
- Live like Jesus.
- Make right choices.
- Resist temptation.

Feet Sandaled with the Gospel of _____
- Stand ready in faith.
- Be at peace with God.
- Be at peace with others.
- Share your faith.

Ed Miller has been at his job for over 20 years, and his hard work has paid off with several promotions. Now his company has offered him a vice-president position. The only catch is that this promotion would require him to move his family across the country.

Ed and Ann are willing to move, but the obstacles are numerous. Their home will be paid off soon. Their oldest son, Jason, is attending college only two hours from their current home. Their daughter Reba—well, she's 16 and in love. She's already told her parents that it would "kill her" to move away from her boyfriend.

On the other hand, the Millers' pastor has a young energetic friend who just planted a church in the area where the Millers would be moving. He would love to have the Millers' leadership skills. And he might connect with Al, the Millers' younger son, who still lives at home but does not attend church. Also, maybe Ed and Ann would have opportunities to share their faith in a more unchurched area.

What would you advise the Millers to do as they face this faith challenge? How might the Enemy want to lead—or rather, mislead—them? How might he attack their faith? In week 4, we will explore the issue of faith. We are saved by grace through faith (Eph. 2:8-9), and with faith we stand against the Enemy.

day *one*

KNOWING WHAT FAITH IS

I once attended the church of a well-known preacher who focuses on healing and spiritual victory. Before the service, people in wheelchairs lined the walls, desperately wanting to be healed. I watched and listened as the preacher challenged the people in the audience to "have faith" so that God would heal them or their loved ones. "Touch the spot that needs healing," he said, "and just believe."

Some time later, the people in the wheelchairs left when I did, still bound by their physical challenges. I wondered how many went home discouraged and

defeated because they thought they didn't have enough faith to be healed. Does this real scenario truly paint a picture of what biblical faith is supposed to be?

In day 1 we'll define faith and consider how to use it as a defensive weapon. Days 2–5 will help you learn to live by faith—even in the middle of spiritual battles.

In Addition to All …

In Ephesians 6:16 the first phrase, "in addition to all," might also be understood as "besides all these" or "in addition to everything else." The point is simple: the first pieces of the armor—the belt of truth, the breastplate of righteousness, and feet sandaled with the gospel of peace—are not complete in themselves. More armor is necessary, and that is the shield of faith. Remember, Paul told believers to wear the *whole* armor of God.

"In addition to all, taking up the shield of faith with which you will be able to extinguish all the flaming arrows of the evil one."
Ephesians 6:16, NASB

God Teaches Us What Faith Is

Hebrews 11:1 provides a simple definition of faith for us: "Faith is the reality of what is hoped for, the proof of what is not seen." Look closely at this definition, and notice just how odd it is. We usually hope for things when we don't have them yet, but faith is the *reality* of what we are hoping for. Proof for us is usually in seeing ("seeing is believing"); but faith is the proof of what we have *not seen*.

Many people enjoy watching courtroom dramas on television. These shows have intriguing investigations, intense interrogation, and riveting courtroom battles, especially when lawyers and police officers use all of their tools and resources to solve a seemingly impossible case.

Can you imagine what would happen if a witness on the stand said something like, "Well, I didn't really see anything; I don't have any proof. I just believe it happened"? Or, "You know, I'm not sure what happened; I'm just hoping so much that I'm right that I'm sure it's reality"? That witness would be torn apart by an opposing lawyer! Still, that sounds like what faith is—"the reality of what is hoped for, the proof of what is not seen."

Here's the difference: faith isn't just someone's opinion or an emotional or unrealistic hope. Faith is "a solid conviction resting on God's words that makes the future present and the invisible seen."[1] Think about it:

- We can't see God, but we still believe He exists because His Word affirms His existence (Gen. 1:1; Heb. 11:6).
- We didn't see God create the world, but we still believe that He did (Gen. 1–2).
- We haven't seen heaven, but we believe in its reality because the Word teaches about it (Rev. 21:1-27).

- We can't see God's presence around us, but we believe that He won't leave us or forsake us (Heb. 13:5).
- We haven't been physically with Jesus, yet we believe with certainty that we will be in the future (John 14:1-3).
- We don't know what tomorrow holds for us, but we know that God controls whatever tomorrow brings (see Luke 12:13-21).

Genuine faith gives substance to our hope and reality to the unseen. When we believe God even when we can't see Him, trust Him even when we can't feel Him, and follow Him even when we aren't certain where He's leading, we're learning to live by faith. That kind of faith stands against the Enemy.

God Gives Us the Shield of Faith

The word translated "shield" in Ephesians 6:16 referred to a large, door-shaped, 4' x 2.5' wooden shield covered with leather. This shield was intended to protect the Roman soldier's entire body, but if we focus only on the type of shield represented here, we will have missed the point. The next activity will show you why.

> **Read the following verses, and briefly describe what each says about a shield.**
>
> Genesis 15:1 _____
>
> Psalm 5:12 _____
>
> Psalm 18:2 _____
>
> Proverbs 30:5 _____

In each of these verses, God is the shield and the refuge. He goes before us, watches over us, and protects us in times of trouble. God takes up the shield and intervenes on our behalf (Ps. 35:2), but Ephesians 6:16 says the shield is the "shield of faith."

> **This lesson is about faith. Is it *God* who protects us in spiritual battles, or is it *faith*? Check one.**
>
> ❏ God protects me in spiritual battles.
> ❏ Faith protects me in spiritual battles.
> ❏ other _____

If you checked one of the first two answers, your answer was incomplete. The answer is *God gives us the faith* that protects us. Don't forget—all of the armor is *His,* and He allows us to wear it in battle. He gives us faith and grows our faith when we hear and follow His Word (Rom. 10:17).

You may recall the story of the Roman centurion (soldier) that is recorded in Matthew 8:5-13. This soldier came to Jesus on behalf of his servant who was dying. Jesus agreed to come and heal him, but the centurion said that Jesus could just speak a word and make it happen. Jesus said to him, "I have not found anyone in Israel with so great a faith!" (v. 10). Where did a Roman soldier get such faith? It certainly wasn't from his pagan background. But he recognized Jesus' authority to heal his servant. God must have given him faith to believe in Jesus.

Or what about the woman with a blood disease who Jesus healed when she touched his garment (Mark 5:25-34)? Where did such a desperate, hurting woman find faith? God surely gave it to her when someone else told her about Jesus (v. 27). Consider the following questions:

- Where did Rahab get faith to side with God's people (Josh. 2)?
- Where did David get his faith to fight Goliath (1 Sam. 17)?
- Where did Elisha get his faith to stand against the Arameans?
  (See 2 Kings 6:15-17.)
- Where did Nehemiah get his faith to build the wall (Neh. 4:14)?

God gave them all faith. In a similar way, He who gives us faith to believe in Jesus also grants us faith to protect us against the Devil's arrows. In no case does God leave us alone to fight the Enemy.

God's Gift of Faith Is a Good Defense

Read Ephesians 6:16 again on page 67. In the ancient world, enemies often shot arrows they tipped with pitch and then set on fire before releasing. These arrows inflicted serious and deadly wounds on armies unprepared for such attacks. Sometimes, armies panicked and simply dropped their burning shields, making themselves more vulnerable to other spears. The best prepared soldiers carried shields with water-soaked leather coverings.

Paul made an important point: the Enemy aims dangerous flaming arrows at believers, but we have faith from God to ward off the attacks. The Enemy's forces are much more powerful than we are, yet those who are "strengthened by the Lord" (Eph. 6:10) can resist and overcome his attacks. This stance is defensive.

As we have learned in previous weeks, one way to overcome the Enemy's attacks involves countering him with the Word of God. Just as Jesus did when He was tempted (Matt. 4:1-11), we can stand on God's Word when under assault. We stand defensively against the Devil by knowing and believing the Word of God.

> The Enemy aims dangerous flaming arrows at believers, but we have faith from God to ward off the attacks.

Match the type of the Enemy's attack on the left with a defensive response from God's Word on the right.

1. ____ discouragement		A. 1 Corinthians 10:13
2. ____ temptation		B. Proverbs 3:5-6
3. ____ false teaching		C. Joshua 1:9
4. ____ persecution		D. 1 John 4:1
5. ____ doubt		E. Matthew 10:28-31

When discouraged, we can trust God and not become dismayed (Josh. 1:9). He has already given us a way to win when we are tempted (1 Cor. 10:13), and He has taught how to recognize false teaching (1 John 4:1). Even if we were to face attacks of persecution, God has taught us how to respond then, too (Matt. 10:28-31). Doubts are resolved when we trust God to show us His way (Prov. 3:5-6). In any of these cases, we stand defensively by knowing and believing God's Word.

Think about how the Enemy attacks you. If his attacks involve any of those just mentioned, read and meditate again on the corresponding biblical text. Consider memorizing it to stand defensively against the Enemy's arrows aimed at you.

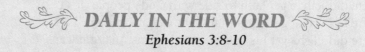

DAILY IN THE WORD
Ephesians 3:8-10

Paul continued to speak about the grace he was given to proclaim to the Gentiles. God gave him grace to proclaim the riches of Christ. The mystery of the gospel—that Jews and Gentiles alike were recipients of God's grace—was revealed. In fact, God shows His wisdom to the evil powers through the unity of the church.

While Paul was given a unique ministry, he didn't think of himself as spiritually superior. Instead, he saw himself as "the least of all the saints" (v. 8). His focus was on the God who created all things. God is fulfilling His plan, and Paul understood his responsibility to proclaim and shed light on the gospel. We have the same responsibility.

APPLICATION
- Ask God to keep you humble as you serve Him.
- If you are at odds with someone in your church, seek forgiveness and unity.

MEMORY VERSE FOR THIS WEEK
"I, therefore, the prisoner in the Lord, urge you to walk worthy of the calling you have received." Ephesians 4:1

Answers to activity on page 69: 1. C; 2. A; 3. D; 4. E; 5. B

day   two

LIVING ON OFFENSIVE FAITH

John serves as an international missionary. Many years ago, he felt God's call to take the gospel to an unreached people group in a distant land. Despite protests from family and friends, John has faithfully followed the Lord's direction in his life. Patrick is a young pastor serving in a small, country church in the southeastern United States. Few people other than family, friends, and those in his church know much about his ministry. Still, he serves diligently, preaching God's Word.

Kathy works as a nurse in a hospital. Every day she seeks opportunities to speak to her patients about God's goodness. Many times she has laid the foundation for a patient's faith in God. Ruby is an older believer who can no longer physically attend church. However, no one in her church prays like she does. Pastor after pastor in her church has felt Ruby's prayer support.

Is each of these believers carrying the shield of faith? Are they marching forward in the spiritual battle? In day 2 we'll learn that carrying the shield of faith is an offensive as well as defensive strategy.

We Are Not Called to Be Fortresses

I am a student of evangelism and church growth. I wholeheartedly believe that the various expressions of the Great Commission in the New Testament (see margin) require us to move out into the world with the gospel. A church standing still can't be obedient to the Great Commission because it's certainly no threat to the Enemy.

I fear some churches have become fortresses. Their members never go out into the community (and the community wouldn't be welcomed if they were to come to the church). Such churches see lost, unchurched people as the opposition. They are driven more by defensively protecting their turf than by offensively fulfilling the Great Commission.

Why do you think some Christians have this fortress mentality?

_____

_____

The problem with becoming a fortress is that the Ephesians 6 passage has a clear offensive element within it. It contains battle imagery, and surely Paul did not expect that believers would only stand still in their armor. Indeed, Ephesians 6:18-20 shows that Paul personally had no intention of standing still; even within a prison cell he was preaching the gospel. Sometimes we best "stand" against the Enemy when we press forward in obedience to deflect the Enemy's arrows (6:11,13-14).

Rate the current state of your church's "fortress mentality" by placing an "x" on the scale.

1	2	3	4	5
We are completely a fortress.	We see others, but don't actively pursue them.	We, the body, are not a fortress.	We plan for and welcome outsiders.	

Faith Is an Action Word

In day 1 we studied the definition of "faith" based on Hebrews 11:1. The eleventh chapter of Hebrews is known as the "Hall of Faith" because it lists biblical characters who lived "by faith."

Read the following verses from Hebrews 11, circling the verbs.

By faith Abel offered to God a better sacrifice than Cain (v. 4).

By faith Noah … in reverence built an ark to deliver his family (v. 7).

"All authority has been given to Me in heaven and on earth. Go, therefore, and make disciples of all nations, baptizing them in the name of the Father and of the Son and of the Holy Spirit, teaching them to observe everything I have commanded you. And remember, I am with you always, to the end of the age."
Matthew 28:18-20

"Go into all the world and preach the gospel to the whole creation."
Mark 16:15

"This is what is written: the Messiah would suffer and rise from the dead the third day, and repentance for forgiveness of sins would be proclaimed in His name to all the nations, beginning at Jerusalem."
Luke 24:46-47

"Peace to you! As the Father has sent Me, I also send you."
John 20:21

"You will receive power when the Holy Spirit has come upon you, and you will be My witnesses in Jerusalem, in all Judea and Samaria, and to the ends of the earth."
Acts 1:8

By faith Abraham … obeyed and went out to a place he was going to receive as an inheritance (v. 8).

By faith Moses … refused to be called the son of Pharaoh's daughter and chose to suffer with the people of God (vv. 24-25).

By faith Rahab the prostitute received the spies in peace and didn't perish with those who disobeyed (v. 31).

All of these biblical models of faith gave evidence of carrying their shields of faith by their actions. You should have circled words like *offered, built, obeyed, went, refused, chose,* and *received*—all action words.

These model believers were not just standing around defending their ground. Their bold confidence in God gave rise to bold initiatives, through which they did whatever God required of them. That kind of faith deflects the Enemy's arrows even as we march forward.

However, faith actions don't come easily. Look again at some of the stories of Hebrews 11. God required Noah to preach coming judgment, and only his family listened to him (v. 7). Abraham's wife Sarah believed God when He promised a son in her old age (v. 11). Moses' obedience included rejecting the pleasures of Egypt in order to identify with his people (vv. 23-27).

Such stories roll on in Hebrews 11. Some heroes of the faith "conquered kingdoms, administered justice, obtained promises, [and] shut the mouths of lions," but still others "were stoned … sawed in two … died by the sword … wandered about in sheepskins, in goatskins, destitute, afflicted, and mistreated" (vv. 33,37). Sometimes carrying the shield of faith means great victory that others will see. At other times victory comes only when we carry the shield to our death. In either case, actions give evidence of our faith.

Actions give evidence of our faith.

Read the previous paragraph again, and check (✔) the statements that best reflect your response.

_____ 1. I'm ready to carry the shield of faith even that means that God requires my death.
_____ 2. I want to carry the shield of faith, but the idea scares me.
_____ 3. I'm more prepared to carry the shield of faith today than before I participated in this study.
_____ 4. I'm not sure that I trust God enough to carry the shield of faith into battle where I might be wounded or killed.
_____ 5. I'm willing to carry the shield of faith to do whatever and to go wherever God leads me.

Faith on the Offensive Follows God Wherever He Directs

Hebrews 11 recalled that Abraham followed God to an unknown land, Moses left Egypt to go to the desert, and Joseph trusted that God would return His people to the promised land. What examples of faith these are for us!

Today we still have models of faith. One of those models for me is a missionary serving in Africa. Not long after he and his family arrived on the field, his small daughter became quite ill. The doctors in his country and a neighboring country decided that she must return to the United States for medical treatment. Her parents brought her to the States, where she received such good medical care that she and her family are now back on the mission field.

I spoke with her missionary dad and asked whether he ever considered keeping his family in the States after his daughter recovered. After all, why return to the place where she had become so ill? I'll never forget his response: "Dr. Lawless," he said, "I never once thought about not going back to my people. In fact, I cried when I asked God to let us go back where we belong. God called us there, and we knew we must go back, even if obedience to Him would be risky for all of us." That's faith on the offensive—going where God asks, regardless of the cost.

Another model for me wasn't a missionary. Instead, John was a faithful church member who told me every year, "Pastor, just tell me where the church needs me this year." Over several years, John served as an assistant Sunday School teacher, deacon yokefellow, trustee, construction team member, outreach leader, drama participant, and pastor's prayer partner. Sometimes the role stretched him, but John was willing to follow God wherever He directed.

How does a parent find sufficient faith to follow God when obedience almost claimed the life of a child? What does it take to be willing to do whatever God asks us to do in His church? God alone must give this kind of faith. In fact, God does give it, for the shield of faith is part of God's armor, not ours. In that armor we can offensively take on the Enemy.

What is the most risky thing that God has called you to do by faith? Why do you think you had the faith to believe?

_____

_____

_____

That's faith on the offensive—going where God asks, regardless of the cost

---

❧ DAILY IN THE WORD ❧
Ephesians 3:11-13

In these verses Paul showed that God has an eternal plan to reach Jews and Gentiles, which He carried out in "the Messiah, Jesus our Lord" (v. 11). Because God fulfilled His purpose in Christ, we now have "boldness, access, and confidence through faith in Him" (v. 12). No other powers are capable of nullifying God's plan.

Indeed, we can trust that God is working His plan, even when it includes suffering (as in Paul's case). We shouldn't become discouraged when we or others we know undergo turmoil. God has a plan to use that suffering. Instead of being disheartened, we should turn to Him in confidence and trust His plan.

APPLICATION
- Put on the pieces of armor that you have learned in this study. Then enter God's presence with boldness in prayer.
- If you question God's purposes in a present circumstance, ask Him to give you confidence in His plans for the future.

MEMORY VERSE FOR THIS WEEK
"I, therefore, the prisoner in the Lord, urge you to walk worthy
of the calling you have received." Ephesians 4:1

day  *three*

FOLLOWING THE EXAMPLE
OF OTHERS

In day 2, I talked about one of my missionary heroes and one of my local church
heroes. I've had so many people—especially laypeople—model faith for me that it's
difficult to list them all.

I think of Mrs. Morgan, who patiently and lovingly trusted God while she cared
for her bedridden husband. Donna, a senior adult, served God faithfully even after
a childhood illness made walking difficult. Jack depended on the faithfulness of
God despite burying a child and grandchild. "Miss Opal" taught children's Sunday
School for decades, always believing that God would "make something out of these
little kids." I am always challenged by faith that says, "I will do whatever God asks,
and I will pay whatever the cost."

The Bible is filled with models of faith whose lives encourage us, strengthen us,
and challenge us. Two of these models are the focus of this lesson. I hope the study
of their lives will increase your faith.

Abraham Modeled Faith Through the Unknown
The first model of faith we will study is Abraham, whose story we have briefly
talked about in earlier lessons.

**Read about Abraham's call to faith in Genesis 12:1-3, and list the
promises God gave him.**

_____

_____

_____

You probably wrote promises such as "I will make you a great nation," "I will bless
you," "I will make your name great," and "I will show you a land." And what about
this promise—"and all the peoples on earth will be blessed through you"? You and
I would be very excited to receive such promises!

Abraham, of course, would pay a heavy price. God told Abraham to leave his
native land, his relatives, and his father's house to find a land that God would show
him. Surely this choice wasn't easy, even if the promises suggested great blessings.

Read the account of Abraham's story in the margin, looking closely at the last phrase.

God promised to show Abraham a land, but the writer of Hebrews says that Abraham started his journey "not knowing where he was going." That phrase raises numerous practical questions:

- How did he know what to pack?
- How did he explain to his wife where they were going?
- How did he explain to relatives why he was leaving?
- How did he know which direction to go?
- How would he know when he finally arrived in the land?

If you were Abraham, challenged to leave without knowing where the journey would take you, how do you think you would react?

Circle any of the following words that might describe your feelings had you been in Abraham's place.

excited   frightened   worried   wondering   trusting

lonely   adventurous   honored   brave   grieved

Regardless of what you circled, we know that Abraham simply obeyed. He stepped out into the unknown, believing in and watching for a place that he had never seen. Doesn't that sound like the definition of faith we studied in day 1?

Abraham believed that he could trust God to keep His Word. Somewhere there would be a land, and somehow there would be a people. The security of God's promises meant more to him than the security of his homeland. Does your shield of faith give you that kind of security?

On a scale of 1-5, with 1 meaning "very unwilling" and 5 meaning "very willing," indicate your willingness to trust God with these unknowns.

_____ 1. God calls you to leave your job because your boss is immoral—but you have no new job.

_____ 2. God calls you to move your family so you can attend seminary in preparation for missionary service.

_____ 3. God calls you to leave your church to help plant a new one in a growing part of town.

_____ 4. God calls you to move to an inner-city area and develop a ministry for people who live there.

_____ 5. God calls you to take out a second mortgage to give to your church's building fund.

A Grieving Father Modeled an Honest Faith

The second model of faith is quite unknown. In fact, some might even question whether he is an example to follow. He is the father of a demon-possessed boy.

Read his story in Mark 9:14-27.

"By faith Abraham, when he was called, obeyed and went out to a place he was going to receive as an inheritance; he went out, not knowing where he was going."
Hebrews 11:8

Many times before, a demon had tormented this man's son, and even Jesus' disciples were unsuccessful in exorcising the evil spirit. When Jesus arrived on the scene, the father said to him, "If You can do anything, have compassion on us and help us" (v. 22). Jesus quickly countered: " 'If You can?' Everything is possible to the one who believes" (v. 23).

Apparently, the faith that had led the father to bring his son to Jesus' disciples in the first place had begun to waver—and why not, when Jesus' own followers could not evict the demon? But Jesus reminded the father that the question was not whether He could heal the boy, but whether the man had faith.

Listen to the father's honest response: "I do believe! Help my unbelief!" (v. 24).

Do you think the father's response was a response of faith?
❑ yes ❑ no

Why or why not?

_____

_____

The father knew that he had confidence in Jesus, but he also knew that his confidence reflected an imperfect faith. He needed Jesus' help to keep his faith current. If Jesus didn't replenish his faith *every second,* the father knew his faith would be eroded by the circumstances of life. In great compassion for and in response to the struggling faith of the grieving father, Jesus commanded the demon to leave the boy (v. 25).

Here's the point for us: we don't simply take up the shield of faith one day and expect it to protect us from that point forward. We can't fight today's battles on the basis of yesterday's power. Carrying the shield means *daily* trusting God and His Word. Of course, that also means daily reading and living His Word.

Furthermore, carrying the shield of faith sometimes means *acting* in faith even when we must cry out with childlike honesty, "Help me, God!" Faith admits the struggle and then wins the battle by turning humbly to God. Faith says, "I will do what God has called me to do, even when it makes no sense to me or frightens me. My minute-by-minute trust in His promises must be my guide. God, I do believe—but help my unbelief!" God not only gives us the shield of faith but also gives us the strength to pick it up.

Where is your faith struggling? What has God called you to do that frightens you? Lead a small group? Witness to a neighbor? Join the choir? Increase your giving? Start attending Sunday School? Go on a mission trip? Share your testimony? Admit a dishonest business practice? Whatever He asks, take the shield of faith even if you must cry out "Lord, help my unbelief!" as you do so.

A Challenge: Who's Watching You?

Just as older generations modeled faith for us, we should be doing the same for the next generations. If your children or grandchildren duplicated your daily walk with God, would you feel blessed or horrified? Because of your model, would they be willing to take a risk for God? Decide now that you will demonstrate how taking up the shield of faith helps you to fend off the Enemy's arrows.

We can't fight today's battles on the basis of yesterday's power.

DAILY IN THE WORD
Ephesians 3:14-19

As Paul brought the theological portion of his book toward a conclusion, he offered a prayer for believers in the Ephesus area. He began by describing the posture of his prayer: "I bow my knees before the Father" (v. 14). Paul bowed himself in humility and approached God with undivided attention.

Paul's prayer didn't focus on the superficial things of this world for which we so often pray. Rather, he began by asking God to grant these believers "power" in the inner man—power that was undoubtedly needed when living in the pagan region around Ephesus. The Holy Spirit gives that strength and power through His indwelling presence. Second, Paul prayed that the Ephesians would comprehend the love of God. This prayer may be one of the more powerful intercessory prayers in all of Scripture.

APPLICATION
- Pray Paul's prayer for three believers today.
- Think about "the breadth and width, height and depth" of God's love for you (Eph. 3:18). Try to comprehend that love.

MEMORY VERSE FOR THIS WEEK
"I, therefore, the prisoner in the Lord, urge you to walk worthy of the calling you have received." Ephesians 4:1

day *four*

UNDERSTANDING ATTACKS ON FAITH

During the Vietnam War, the Viet Cong fighters dug miles of underground tunnels for protection and secret transportation. Some of these tunnels were large enough to store tanks. Often the enemy's tunnels were so well-concealed that American soldiers camped directly above them, not knowing the activity underground.

The Devil attacks believers today, seemingly out of nowhere. Subtly, he undercuts our faith and challenges our trust in God, and we don't always recognize his attacks. In day 4 we'll learn to recognize two ways the Enemy attacks our faith. When we know some of his schemes, we are better prepared to use the shield of faith effectively.

The Enemy Attacks Faith Through Worry

Read Matthew 6:25-34 below, and circle any words or phrases that challenge us not to worry.

This is why I tell you: Don't worry about your life, what you will eat or what you will drink; or about your body, what you will wear. Isn't life more than food and the body more than clothing? Look at the birds of the sky: they don't sow or reap or gather into barns, yet your heavenly Father feeds them. Aren't you worth more than they? Can any of you add a single cubit to his height by worrying? And why do you worry about clothes? Learn how the wildflowers of the field grow: they don't labor or spin thread. Yet I tell you that not even Solomon in all his splendor was adorned like one of these! If that's how God clothes the grass of the field, which is here today and thrown into the furnace tomorrow, won't He do much more for you—you of little faith? So don't worry, saying, "What will we eat?" or "What will we drink?" or "What will we wear?" For the idolaters eagerly seek all these things, and your heavenly Father knows that you need them. But seek first the kingdom of God and His righteousness, and all these things will be provided for you. Therefore don't worry about tomorrow, because tomorrow will worry about itself. Each day has enough trouble of its own.

The phrases "don't worry" and "why do you worry?" echo throughout these words of Jesus. Jesus said that the Father who takes care of the birds, gives beauty to the wildflowers, and grows the grass will take care of His children. So what is the point of worry? It seems fairly simple, doesn't it?

Yet, sometimes we are consumed by the very worry Jesus spoke against, exactly what the Enemy wants. Notice how Satan subtly attacks:
- He wants us to focus more on temporary—not eternal—things (v. 25).
- He wants us to think worry will somehow make a difference (v. 27).
- He wants us to think that somehow God Himself doesn't know what we need (v. 32; see also 6:8).
- He wants us to be consumed with the possibilities that have not yet happened; that is, he wants us to be worried about tomorrow (v. 34).

Think about your current worries. Are you worrying about temporary things or things that won't matter in eternity? Is your worry adding one moment to your life, or might it be shortening your life? Does your worry imply that God doesn't know what you need or that He is unwilling to meet your need? Are you worried more about current reality or about what you think might happen?

Where do you believe God is when you're worried? Worry, by definition, is a lack of faith in God. It is, as one writer has said, "practical atheism."[2] In fact worry quickly becomes idolatry of the self: I am more concerned about myself than I am about trusting God's purposes. When we are at such a point, we aren't carrying the shield of faith.

Check (✔) the statements that most closely reflect your life.

_____ 1. I don't worry about anything.
_____ 2. I worry about some things, but I don't let them consume me.

_____ 3. I worry but only about important things.

_____ 4. I worry too much about too many things.

_____ 5. Worry sometimes so consumes me that I shut down.

If worry is a problem for you, ask God to help you to trust Him. We only trust people or things that prove to be faithful. The Enemy stakes his battle plan on your worry. It will rob you of faith and cause you to fall victim to him. Take up the shield of faith and stand against this scheme of the Enemy in your life.

Worry	vs.	**Faith**
focuses on circumstances and self obsesses about what might happen based on our thoughts		focuses on God trusts what God has and will do based on God's Word
elevates the temporary over the eternal keeps us awake at night		sees the eternal despite the temporary gives us sleep at night
is a tool of the Enemy		is a gift of God

The Enemy Attacks Faith Through Fear and Doubt

Picture this: you are with Jesus' disciples in a boat in the middle of a storm. About 3:00 a.m. you see what appears to be a ghost walking toward the boat. Wouldn't you, like the rest of the disciples, be frightened (Matt. 14:22-26)? The "ghost," though, was Jesus, and He told His disciples not to fear (v. 27). Would you have followed Peter's lead and asked Jesus for permission to come to Him on the water (v. 28)? Quite possibly, Peter had more faith than most of us would have had.

Peter walked on the water toward Jesus (v. 29)—at least, that is, until he sensed the strength of the wind. Gripped by fear, Peter began to sink (v. 30). Jesus questioned him about his little faith (v. 31). Rather quickly, Peter changed from a man of faith walking on the water to a man of doubt sinking in the sea.

The word translated as "doubt" in Matthew 14:31 implies the idea of one person trying to go in two different directions at once. The same idea appears in James 1:6, where James teaches that those who pray must do so believing and not doubting. The picture is not of one who simply struggles with weak faith, yet believes (like the father of the demon-possessed boy in yesterday's lesson) but of one who is double-minded. In one moment he prays, and in the next moment he completely doubts.

Only the grace of God saves us when we so waver. One minute we believe, and the next minute we doubt. For one moment we are strong, but then we are suddenly weak. What happens to make the difference? Most of the time, the same thing happens to us that happened to Peter—we get more focused on our circumstances than on the God who is bigger than our circumstances!

I well remember a time in my life when I wrongly focused on the events of life. My wife and I had decided to return to school, and we put our house on the market in preparation for our move. School started, and we moved—but our house didn't sell. For many months, we faced paying both a mortgage and rent.

At least for a while, I worried, doubted, and feared. I was afraid that we would lose all of our savings. I worried that we would need to rely on parents and close friends to pay our bills. At times I doubted whether God was hearing my prayers. And, in the midst of all of my fretting, I took my eyes off the God who had never before let us down. I temporarily forgot about His long-term, constant care and faithfulness because I was so afraid our home would never sell. My shield of faith was down—even though I was a seminary student preparing to teach others about faith. For too long, the Enemy won in my life through fear and doubt.

God, of course, met our needs, but He did so in His time and in His way. I can only wonder now how much joy and peace I lost while I doubted and feared, choosing not to take up the shield of faith.

Think about a situation in your life when fear or doubt harmed your relationship with God. What did that teach you?

_____

_____

_____

If you're facing such a time right now, pray and ask God to give you His grace to take up the shield of faith.

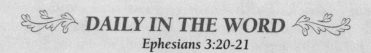

DAILY IN THE WORD
Ephesians 3:20-21

Paul concluded the first division of Ephesians with a doxology, or a statement of glory or praise that one gives to God. The doxology flows smoothly from the preceding prayer in verses 14-19. The Messiah's love surpasses knowledge (v. 19), and God is "able to do above and beyond all that we ask or think" (v. 20). God's love and power eclipse anything we can imagine.

As Paul praised God, he echoed the theme that permeates the Book of Ephesians—God's awesome power. God's power redeemed us and works within us, and that same power can win spiritual battles. We as His church are to give Him glory forever.

APPLICATION
  • Praise God for His power.
  • Trust that God is strong enough to help you overcome anything you face this week.

MEMORY VERSE FOR THIS WEEK
"I, therefore, the prisoner in the Lord, urge you to walk worthy of the calling you have received." Ephesians 4:1

day *five*

INCREASING OUR FAITH

When you were in school, do you remember the student who asked, "What's the test gonna be like?" five minutes after the teacher answered that question? As a professor, I wonder if students like this one are in the same universe as me, much less in the same classroom. Yet, because I am called to teach, I long for some way to reach that student. To be honest, I wish I could simply unscrew the top of his head, pour in the information that he needs, put the top of his head back in place, and send him on his way. But I haven't found a shortcut to learning.

The same can be said about faith. I wish we could write a lesson that provides a simple way to increase our faith—perhaps by our small-group leaders and pastors just pouring faith into our heads and hearts. As we learned yesterday, the Enemy fights against the process too much for it to be that easy.

Despite this spiritual battle, in day 5 we'll learn some general guidelines of taking up the shield of faith. Keep in mind that this task is not intended to be easy.

Faith Comes by Hearing the Word of God

Depending on which version of the Bible you are using, Romans 10:17 probably looks something like one of these:

"So faith comes from what is heard, and what is heard comes through the message about Christ" (HCSB).

"So faith comes from hearing, and hearing by the word of Christ" (NASB).

"Consequently, faith comes from hearing the message, and the message is heard through the word of Christ" (NIV).

Regardless of your translation, these teachings are clear. First, faith is not separated from hearing the message of the Scriptures. In some mysterious way, God awakens our hearts and makes our faith possible when we hear the Word. Second, the Word that we hear is the Word of Christ. The good news about Christ, proclaimed by His messengers, leads us to faith. In that sense, the process is circular: we hear God's Word, and He produces faith in us so that we might respond in faith to the Word that we have heard.

It's no wonder, then, that Paul had previously asked in the same chapter of Romans, "How can they call on Him in whom they have not believed? And how can they believe without hearing about Him? And how can they hear without a preacher?" (Rom. 10:14). Faith doesn't happen apart from hearing the Word of God.

Think about all you've learned thus far in the Book of Ephesians. What teachings have already strengthened your faith? You should have underlined them or placed a star beside them.

If not, go back and highlight them in some way. Be prepared to share them with your small group.

Faith Comes by Trusting the Word

How do we know we can trust God? What promises has He given us? What commands call on us to trust Him?

Read and briefly summarize each of the following verses that inspire us to trust God.

Genesis 15:1 _____

Deuteronomy 20:1 _____

Joshua 1:9 _____

Isaiah 41:10 _____

Jeremiah 46:27 _____

Luke 2:10 _____

Hebrews 13:6 _____

What do these verses have in common? All include some version of the most common command in the Scriptures: "Do not be afraid." In most cases, the command is accompanied by this marvelous promise that alleviates our fears: "I am with you."

Why do you suppose God gave this command so many times through His inspired writers unless He knew how often we would be afraid? Remember, the Enemy undercuts our faith by fear and worry—but God reminds us again and again that He is with us, and nothing is strong enough to be against us (Rom. 8:31). Our faith grows when we trust that no one's strength can stand against His strength.

> "What then are we to say about these things? If God is for us, who is against us?"
> *Romans 8:31*

Faith Comes by Living the Word

Jake had been a Christian for many years, but he had never faced anything like this. His job was unexpectedly gone. His wife was facing health problems. His oldest son was rebelling. The bills were piling up. Jake did the only thing he knew to do—he pleaded with God to give him faith to endure these struggles.

When do we most often want God to increase our faith? In what circumstances do we try hard to take up the shield of faith? Typically, we cry out for more faith when we're facing a situation beyond our control—when we realize that we need God's help. Certainly, there's nothing wrong with seeking faith at times like these. Sometimes desperation rightly turns us to God and His Word. However, we need to ask some more basic questions: In addition to seeking God and faith in difficult times, am I trusting Him in faith in usual times? Do I live by faith even when life is going smoothly? Do I, for example …

> When do we most often want God to increase our faith?

- trust Him enough to tithe?
- trust Him to take the risk of telling my neighbor about Him?
- believe in His power enough to turn from my habitual sins?
- have the confidence in Him that I need to teach a Bible study class or small group?

- believe in the power of His Word enough to read it every day?
- so trust His existence that I speak to Him daily through prayer?

Why should God trust us with more faith when we are not faithful to the Word that He has already given us? You see, God will increase our faith only when we obediently follow what we already know of His Word. To put it more simply, God expects us to be wearing the breastplate of righteousness *and* carrying the shield of faith. The pieces of the armor can't be separated from each other. It's a package deal.

Only through living in faith—that is, by trusting God even when we can't see Him—do we wear the belt of truth, the breastplate of righteousness, or have our feet sandaled with the gospel of peace. When we live by faith we are equipped and deployed for spiritual warfare.

Check (✔) each statement that reflects your daily Christian walk.

❑ I'm reading God's Word faithfully.
❑ I'm learning to live more and more like Jesus.
❑ I'm gaining victory over sins in my life.
❑ I'm not only turning from wrong but truly repenting of it.
❑ I'm more disciplined in reading God's Word and praying.
❑ I'm more willing to stand firmly on my faith, even if I stand alone.
❑ I've been telling others about Jesus.
❑ I'm at peace with God.
❑ I'm at peace with others.
❑ I'm knowing, living, and trusting God's Word.
❑ I'm willing to take greater risks for God if that's what He requires.

A Review: Wearing the Full Armor of God

Do you see how all the armor pieces are interrelated—and thus, why Paul said that we must wear the full armor of God? Consider these connections:

- Wearing the belt of truth means knowing and living the Word of God.
- Wearing the breastplate of righteousness also requires knowing and living the Word of God. The Word reveals God's standards of righteousness for us.
- We experience God's peace only when we both know Him and follow Him faithfully.
- When we know God's peace, we stand firmly and march forward to tell others about Him.
- Standing firmly and marching forward demand that we carry the shield of faith.
- Carrying the shield of faith requires hearing, knowing, believing, and living God's Word (Rom. 10:17).

DAILY IN THE WORD
Ephesians 4:1-6

We've learned that Paul divided Ephesians into two major sections. In the first three chapters, he focused on laying a theological foundation while the last three chapters applied these truths practically.

The transition between the two sections is clear in Ephesians 4:1 (the memory verse for this week). Paul expected the doctrinal truths in Ephesians 1–3 to make a difference in the way the Ephesians lived.

The theme of "walking" is important throughout Ephesians 4–6. "Walking" in Christ is characterized by humility, gentleness, patience, accepting love, and peacekeeping. Christians are to be "one" (a term used seven times in these verses), following the one true God who is Father, Son, and Spirit.

APPLICATION
- Evaluate your life in the light of these verses. Turn from any arrogance, impatience, or ungodly intolerance.
- Pray this prayer: "Lord, help me to walk worthy of my calling."

MEMORY VERSE FOR THIS WEEK
"I, therefore, the prisoner in the Lord, urge you to walk worthy of the calling you have received." Ephesians 4:1

1. R. Kent Hughes, *Hebrews: Volume Two* in *Preaching the Word* (Wheaton, IL: Crossway Books, 1993), 60.
2. Robert H. Mounce, *Matthew* (Peabody, MA: Hendrickson, 1991), 61.

Case Study

A state leader speaks during a missions rally held at your church. His emotions and passion are gripping as he describes the millions of nonbelievers in his state—and then shows that there are very few evangelical churches there. "Help us plant more churches," he pleads.

At your church's next business meeting, a lay leader stands to say, "I believe God wants our church to give sacrificially toward planting churches in that state. I move that we add to our budgeted missions giving so that a church plant there receives 5 percent of our undesignated offerings for the next three years."

Quickly, another leader speaks. "I'm all for missions, but we need to think before spending that kind of money on a new church that may or may not survive. Our budget is so tight now that we're just getting by. There's a fine line between faith and foolishness, and I think the Devil wants us to lean toward foolishness."

"I don't disagree that there's a fine line," says the man who proposed the motion, "but I think our problem is that we do too little by faith. What have we done lately that is so God-sized that we can't take credit for it? Even if this challenge really stretches our budget, we need to move forward in faith."

Although you probably need more information, would you likely vote for the motion to set aside 5 percent of the church's offerings to support a church plant? How would faith factor into your decision? Do you think your current church would vote in favor or against this motion?

What is your church doing that is so "God-sized" the Enemy has probably taken note? Write it (them) in the margin.

Deflecting Worry

In each arrow write one specific worry you are experiencing. (If you are not worried about anything personally, develop your list for believers in general.) In the shield next to each worry, write a character trait of God that will strengthen faith in Him and deflect the flaming arrows of worry.

WORRY	CHARACTER TRAIT OF GOD

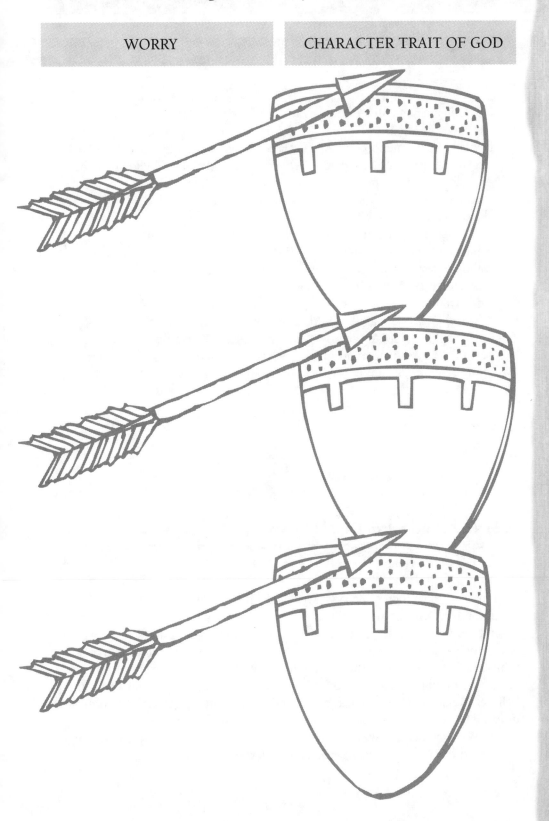

The Helmet of Salvation

REVIEWING THE FULL ARMOR OF GOD

Belt of _____
- Know Jesus.
- Know His Word.
- Live the Word.

Breastplate of _____
- Live like Jesus.
- Make right choices.
- Resist temptation.

Feet Sandaled with the Gospel of _____
- Stand ready in faith.
- Be at peace with God.
- Be at peace with others.
- Share your faith.

Shield of _____
- Know and live the Word of God.
- Act on your faith.
- Resist worry, fear, and doubt.
- Trust the promises of God.

Not long after the Miller family made their move across the country, they faced a crisis like they had never experienced. Ann's father, whom the family adored, unexpectedly died in an automobile accident. For Ann, this tragedy became a crisis of faith. "Why," she asked, "did God take my father? And why did He move us so far from my family when He knew they would need me?" She even briefly questioned the goodness of a God who would allow such tragedies to happen.

At her father's funeral, Ann found comfort in support from her parents' church and in the minister's words about eternal life and heaven. She believed without question she would see her father again. Still, her heart hurt. "I know I have hope for the future," she thought, "but what about hope for today when I'm hurting so badly?"

The Enemy did all he could to rob Ann of her joy in the Lord. This week we'll learn about the hope God gives us as we take up the helmet of salvation. God's grace in our lives gives us a present-tense assurance and future-tense hope simply because we are His children.

day *one*

UNDERSTANDING WHO WE WERE

I am married to an incredible lady. My wife Pam was reared in a Christian home where God and church were central. For those of you who remember these mission organizations, she participated in Girls in Action and Acteens. In fact, she was an Acteen queen with a scepter and a cape! When we married, in addition to being the minister's wife, she sang in the choir and taught in Sunday School, GAs, Acteens, and Vacation Bible School. Although quiet and gentle, Pam is the most faithful believer I know. In fact, it's hard for me to think of Pam as ever being a nonbeliever or lost. Maybe you know someone who fits this same description.

The Bible is clear, however, that all of us—no matter how righteous we might seem apart from Christ—have sinned and fallen short of God's glory (Rom. 3:23).

As we learned briefly in week 3, without Christ we have no hope; we all face a bleak eternity. That's why salvation is so important.

This week we'll study the helmet of salvation, the fifth piece of the armor of God. The goal is to help you appreciate and live out the blessings of salvation, realizing that a better understanding of these truths will help you stand in victory.

Today's study focuses on our condition prior to meeting Christ. It might seem odd to start there, but when we realize how lost we really were, we can best appreciate what God has done for us.

Do We Take or Receive the Helmet of Salvation?

Read the two Scripture verses in the margin. In the first one, God is wearing the helmet of salvation. In the second, believers are instructed to wear the helmet. Paul most assuredly was thinking of the first verse when he wrote Ephesians 6:17. What did he mean, then, when he told us to "take" the helmet of salvation?

Answering this question is easier if we know that the word translated "take" in Ephesians 6:17 can also be understood as "accept" or "receive." Just as a soldier was to take his helmet from an officer in charge of supplies, we take the helmet of salvation by receiving it from God. He is both the "source and perfecter of our faith" (Heb. 12:2). The importance of this truth—that God is the originator, the protector, and the finisher of our faith—will become even more evident as we consider our condition prior to meeting Christ.

> "He [God] put on righteousness like a breastplate, and a helmet of salvation on His head." *Isaiah 59:17*

> "Take the helmet of salvation." *Ephesians 6:17*

We Were Blinded by the Enemy

We learned in week 3 that nonbelievers are blinded by the Enemy, but in those five days of studies we were thinking more about others we're trying to reach for Christ. Now, we must remember that we, too, were once blinded. We could easily insert our own names in this text:

"Regarding [_____]: the god of this age has blinded the minds of the unbelievers so they cannot see the light of the gospel of the glory of Christ" (2 Cor. 4:4).

The Enemy once ruled over us, and he had successfully clouded our minds to keep us from believing the gospel. That isn't to say that we bear no responsibility, for we are all sinners by nature (Rom. 5:12,19) and by our actions (Rom. 3:23; Col. 1:21). We were alienated from God and hostile toward Him. In the end, we served the Enemy when we were nonbelievers.

In the book *Out of Their Faces and into Their Shoes,* John Kramp writes about "lostology," or the study of being lost. The author's point is that in order for us to be good Christian witnesses, we need to understand spiritually lost people around us. For example, most lost people don't mind being lost; in fact, they like it because that's their nature.[1] Maybe one way we can understand lost people is to recall that we, too, were once lost and blinded by the Enemy.

Check each statement that reflects your thoughts about the truths in day 1 so far.

_____ 1. I'm not sure that I served the Enemy when I was a nonbeliever.
_____ 2. I was a good person even though I didn't know Christ personally.
_____ 3. I know that I served the Enemy, and I'm grateful for God's grace.
_____ 4. It's hard for me to recall the way I lived before becoming a Christian.
_____ 5. I've never thought about the fact that I was blinded by Satan prior to my becoming a Christian.
_____ 6. I'm not yet certain that I'm a Christian; I may still be serving the Enemy.

We Were in the "Domain of Darkness"

In Colossians 1:9-14, Paul expressed a powerful prayer for the believers in Colosse (in fact, this prayer is a good one to memorize).

Read this prayer in your Bible.

Within this prayer, the apostle described our condition before we trusted Christ: we were in the "domain of darkness" (1:13). Compare that verse to Jesus' words to Paul when He called him to be a missionary: "I will rescue you from the people and from the Gentiles, to whom I now send you, to open their eyes that they may turn from darkness to light and from the power of Satan to God" (Acts 26:17-18).

Nonbelievers are held under Satan's power in the kingdom of darkness. The Enemy is the ruler of a kingdom, and we, by our nature and by our subsequent choices to reject God, chose to be subjects of that kingdom.

Read each of the Scriptures in the margin, and underline the words that describe the state of nonbelievers prior to salvation.

Needless to say, the pictures painted by these texts aren't positive. Jesus came as the light, and many rejected Him. In fact, some loved the darkness more than light because "their deeds were evil" (John 3:19). In our lostness we, too, lived in the dark, blinded and controlled by the Enemy.

We Were in Bondage to Satan's Influence

In week 3, we studied Ephesians 2:1-3. Read verses 1-2 below, and underline the words you think refer to your spiritual state before you became a Christian. Circle the words you think refer to Satan or his influence.

You were dead in your trespasses and sins in which you previously walked according to this worldly age, according to the ruler of the atmospheric domain, the spirit now working in the disobedient.

"Life was in Him, and that life was the light of men. That light shines in the darkness, yet the darkness did not overcome it."
John 1:4-5

"This, then, is the judgment: the light has come into the world, and people loved darkness rather than the light because their deeds were evil. For everyone who practices wicked things hates the light and avoids it, so that his deeds may not be exposed."
John 3:19-20

"You were once darkness, but now you are light in the Lord. Walk as children of light."
Ephesians 5:8

"You are a 'chosen race, a royal priesthood, a holy nation, a people for His possession, so that you may proclaim the praises' of the One who called you out of darkness into His marvelous light."
1 Peter 2:9

You probably underlined "dead in your trespasses and sins." Did you circle "the ruler of the atmospheric domain" and "the spirit now working in the disobedient"? Both phrases refer to Satan. The one who rules the air also works in the lives of the disobedient. The Enemy fights to keep individuals in darkness.

How is Satan "now working in the disobedient"? First, he makes sin look inviting. The Enemy dangles temptation in front of us while covering up the consequences if we give in. Indeed, sin *is* often fun—albeit only temporarily—and we take the Enemy's bait over and over again. Second, he gives non-Christians lies to believe. Consider some of them you may have heard: "I'm good enough to go to heaven." "There must be more than one way to God." "There is no God."

Maybe you know someone like Bobby, who is deeply interested in "spiritual things." Whenever I talk to him, he brings up something related to religion. The more I talk to him, though, the more I realize how far he is from Christ. He believes in multiple ways to God, and he sees no room for telling others how to believe. Bobby has bought into the lies of the Enemy yet thinks of himself as spiritual.

The Enemy's strategy is simple. He invites nonbelievers to enjoy their sin while also holding on to lies that soothe their consciences. This choice results only in continued and deeper darkness.

More In-Depth Study

For each of the Enemy's lies, write a biblical truth response. Then, find the verse in the New Testament that best reflects your response. The first one has been completed for you.

LIE	RESPONSE	SCRIPTURE
"There are multiple ways to God."	Jesus is the only way to God.	John 14:6
"You can always wait until tomorrow to follow God."		
"There is no God."		
"A loving God won't allow anyone to go to hell."		
"You're good enough to get to heaven."		

The End of the Story?

If this lesson were the end of the story, nonbelievers would be in a desperate situation. The spiritual battle would be lost, and none of us would have any hope. I recently asked members of a church in the Northeast to describe their lives before meeting Christ. They used the words *hopeless, unhappy, anxious, guilty, purposeless, pointless,* and *dark.* They now see their former lives through a Christian lens, but their descriptions were accurate. Consider how separated from God you were prior to salvation—even if you didn't realize it at the time. Humbly thank God for allowing you to receive the helmet of salvation. If you're not yet a follower of Christ, turn to page 147 of this member book and review the steps to salvation. Talk to your small-group leader about your desire to become a Christian.

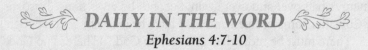

DAILY IN THE WORD
Ephesians 4:7-10

Today's reading includes some of the most controversial verses in the Book of Ephesians. Paul stated that the Messiah "ascended" and "descended to the lower parts of the earth" (vv. 8-9). Paul most likely spoke of Christ's ascension into heaven at the conclusion of His earthly ministry. The controversial phrase concerns Jesus' descent. Some scholars argue that this phrase refers to Christ's coming to earth. Others claim a reference to Christ's burial, while still others believe that Christ descended into hell for a period of time after His death and before His resurrection.

The primary point to remember, though, is that Christ ascended. He who came to earth has taken captive the powers and has authority over all things. This same Messiah graciously gives us gifts and power to fulfill our calling.

APPLICATION
- Thank God that Jesus rules over any power that might threaten you.
- Work with your church leaders to determine how God might want you to fulfill your calling in your congregation.

MEMORY VERSE FOR THIS WEEK
"Be kind and compassionate to one another, forgiving one another, just as God also forgave you in Christ." Ephesians 4:32

day two

UNDERSTANDING
WHAT GOD DID

Several years ago, my wife and I decided to build a home rather than purchase one already built. (Does this very idea bring back bad memories for you?) We were excited about the idea, but we had no idea all that would be involved in the process.

Finding a piece of property. Choosing a house plan. Changing the house plan as we wanted. Deciding whether to finish the basement. Changing the house plan again! Adding a bonus room. Changing the house plan one more time. Adding more electrical outlets. Picking the colors of paint, styles of light fixtures, and type of carpet. Deciding what landscaping we wanted. Determining the type of front door we wanted. Ordering the appliances. Doing a walk-through to make final changes—final, at least, until we moved in and wanted more changes.

We changed our minds so many times that I'm sure out builder sometimes wondered if our business was worth the hassle. We had an original building plan, but we assumed that it was always subject to our revision. How grateful I am that God's plan for our salvation has always been completely settled!

Day 1 ended with nonbelievers in trouble. They were blinded by the Enemy, held in the domain of darkness, and bound up in the Enemy's influences. Today we will learn the good news: God has always had a plan to deal with this problem.

God's Word Shows Us That He Has a Plan

To be honest, I intentionally told you only part of the story yesterday. Several of the same Scriptures that show the state of nonbelievers also give hope for those who do believe. The first activity for today will show you some of these texts.

Read each of the verses. Then, summarize the verses listed under "complete" to see God's plan.

READ

COMPLETE

1. John 1:5—"That light shines in the darkness, yet the darkness did not overcome it …

John 1:12— _____

_____

_____."

2. Acts 26:18a—"to open their eyes that they may turn from darkness to light and from the power of Satan to God …

Acts 26:18b— _____

_____

_____."

3. Ephesians 2:1—"And you were dead in your trespasses and sins …

Ephesians 2:4-5— _____

_____

_____."

4. Colossians 1:13—"He has rescued us from the domain of darkness and transferred us into the kingdom of the Son He loves …

Colossians 1:14— _____

_____

_____."

The rest of the story is the best part. Though others reject the light of Christ, God gives believers the privilege of being called His children. He rescued us from Satan's power so He could forgive our sins. We were dead in our trespasses, but He loved us and made us alive through His Son. He transferred us into His kingdom, granting us redemption and forgiveness. The Enemy works hard to keep nonbelievers in darkness, but he is no match for the God who has a plan to overcome him.

> The Enemy is no match for the God who has a plan to overcome him.

God's Plan Required Death

As early as Genesis 3, God's Word shows that He had a plan to destroy the Enemy. Announcing His judgment on the serpent, God said, "I will put hostility between you and the woman, and between your seed and her seed. He will strike your head, and you will strike his heel" (3:15). Although some debate the interpretation of this verse, many scholars believe this judgment is the first announcement of God's good news. Someone from the seed of woman would strike the head of the serpent (which would kill the serpent), but the serpent would wound the seed of the woman in the process.

The seed of the woman is best understood as Jesus. The serpent—Satan (2 Cor. 11:3; Rev. 12:9)—wounded Jesus on the cross, but the Enemy didn't win there. Through His death on the cross, Jesus destroyed the power of the serpent (Col. 2:15). How did Jesus' death accomplish that victory?

Jesus paid the price for our sin. The penalty for sin has always been death (Gen. 2:15-17). In some mysterious way, Jesus bore our sins on the cross (Isa. 53:6,12) and paid the penalty for our sin. As a result, we can be declared righteous through Jesus' death (Rom. 5:9-11).

Look how Paul described this transaction in one of his letters to the Corinthians. As you read, underline the phrases that contain good news.

He made the One who did not know sin to be sin for us, so that we might become the righteousness of God in Him (2 Cor. 5:21).

Did you underline the entire passage? We may not fully understand God's plan, yet how can we not see it as good news?

Jesus took upon Himself God's wrath for our sin. Several New Testament Scriptures refer to Jesus' death as a "propitiation" for sins (Rom. 3:25; Heb. 2:17; 1 John 2:2; 1 John 4:10). The word *propitiation* means "a sacrifice that bears God's wrath to the end and in so doing changes God's wrath toward us into favor."[2] God, who is absolutely holy, poured out on Jesus His anger over sin, and this abated His anger toward us.

Think about it—God put on His own Son the anger that we so deserve. Christ became a curse for us so that we would not be cursed anymore (Gal. 3:13). The Enemy and his tempting offers are no match for that kind of love!

But if God's plan had ended with Jesus in the grave, what hope would we have? Paul said our "faith is worthless" and we are "still in [our] sins" (1 Cor. 15:17) if Jesus wasn't raised from the dead. The Enemy would have won in that case.

That, of course, is not the case. Three days after His death, Jesus—the One who had said that He was the "resurrection and the life" (John 11:25)—rose from the dead (Matt. 28:1-10). We will look at this hope that God gives us later this week.

Many years ago, I traveled to Israel for the first time. I was a fairly young Christian, and I couldn't wait to get to Calvary where Jesus was crucified. Scholars debate the actual location, but one proposed site was just behind a busy, noisy bus station. Thousands of people came and went each day, never stopping to think about the eternal events that may have occurred not far from the station. I judged them harshly then, but I've since learned that we're all guilty of hurrying through life and neglecting the cross. Appreciating the helmet of salvation means that we must again slow down and look at the cross.

God's Plan Demands Our Response

Remember, this entire study assumes that wearing the full armor of God is about *how we live*. We learned last week that *faith* is an action word; we will act on our faith if we truly believe. Consider some ways that wearing the helmet of salvation must affect the way we live each day. We will:

- love Him with our actions and our words;
- reject the Enemy's offers because God's offer of love and forgiveness means more than anything he offers; that is, we will wear the breastplate of righteousness;
- want to read God's Word because we want to hear from the holy One who has made us His children; we will want to know His truth in order to wear the belt of truth;
- look forward to times of prayer, knowing that His truth and righteousness in us make prayer more meaningful and fruitful;
- want to trust God for eternity, for He alone has the words of eternal life (John 6:68); in Him and His promises we take up the shield of faith.

Meditate on God's plan to save us when we were in bondage to the Enemy. Look at the other images describing Christ's death listed in the margin. List a few words that describe your thoughts or feelings as you consider the helmet of salvation we receive from God.

_____

_____

_____

_____

OTHER IMAGES OF THE DEATH OF JESUS
- A redemption from bondage (Mark 10:45)
- A reconciliation (2 Cor. 5:18-19)
- A sacrifice for sins (Heb. 9:26)
- A substitution (1 Pet. 2:24)

DAILY IN THE WORD
Ephesians 4:11-16

In this Scripture passage, Paul specifically mentioned some people, or "gifts," the Messiah gave to the church. The apostles, prophets, evangelists, and pastor/teachers were given "for the training of the saints in the work of ministry" (v. 12). The trained believers do ministry that builds up the church, help members mature and stabilize in their faith, and promote unity in the church. Mature believers will then recognize false teachings and will not be "tossed … by every wind of teaching" (v. 14).

Mature believers speak "the truth in love" (v. 15), encouraging and challenging one another to grow in every way in Christ. Again, Paul called on this diverse group of believers to support one another as each played his or her individual role in the body.

APPLICATION
- Thank God for the people He has given your church.
- Evaluate your Christian growth, looking for areas in which you are not growing as you should.

MEMORY VERSE FOR THIS WEEK
"Be kind and compassionate to one another, forgiving one another, just as God also forgave you in Christ." Ephesians 4:32

day  *three*

UNDERSTANDING WHO WE ARE IN CHRIST

Let's start today's study with an activity. For each of the following statements, indicate your level of agreement or disagreement, with 1 being "strongly disagree" and 5 being "strongly agree."

_____ 1. I'm a child of God.
_____ 2. I'm a new creation.
_____ 3. I'm created in God's image.
_____ 4. I'm a coheir with Christ.
_____ 5. God has prepared good works for me to do.

How did you respond to the statements? If you're a Christian, you should have at least agreed with each one (see John 1:12; 2 Cor. 5:17; Gen. 1:27; Rom. 8:16-17; Eph. 2:8-10). We are created in God's image and thus are coheirs with Christ. As God's children, we are new creations prepared for good works. We are unique and special to God.

But the Enemy doesn't want us to know these truths. Instead, he capitalizes on false messages that we've heard so we don't experience joy in serving God. You've probably heard some of the messages listed in the margin.

Day 3 focuses on reminding us who we are in Christ by looking at people touched by Jesus. When we understand who we are in Jesus, we best seize the helmet of salvation and prepare to enter the spiritual battle.

FALSE MESSAGES YOU MAY HAVE HEARD
- "God will never love you again."
- "God won't forgive you for what you did."
- "You will never change."
- "You will never be worth anything."
- "You can never overcome your past."
- "Nobody will ever love you."

First, A Caution …

When we study who we are in Christ, we will face the inherent danger of having spiritual arrogance. Somehow, our focus shifts from God's graciousness to our goodness. The Enemy wins when that kind of shift takes place.

This week's studies are organized specifically to avoid this shift. In days 1–2 we began with a look at how desperately blind we are apart from Christ, followed by a lesson on God's plan for us. Only now are we ready to talk about who we are in Christ—after we've learned that *only* God's lovingkindness has rescued us from the Enemy's clutches. We would not be *in Christ* had God not first loved us while we were sinners (Rom. 5:8).

In Christ, We Are Loved

I remember the first verse I ever memorized as a new, 13-year-old Christian—John 3:16. My pastor told me, "This is how we know that God loved us. He gave His only Son to die for us, and He will give us eternal life if we believe in Him." I was amazed then by God's love, and I'm still amazed over 30 years later.

Among other things, I'm amazed that Jesus loves the unlovable. Have you ever met people who were hard to love until Jesus saved them? I changed their names to protect the guilty, but I remember several I've met:
- Judith, the woman who tried to catch a pastor in a web of immorality.
- Rebecca, whose rotten attitude made people intentionally avoid her.
- Chandra, the divorcée who blamed everything on her ex-husband.
- Charlie, the rapist.
- Chris, who flaunted his wealth all over town.

All of these were unlovable, and yet Jesus gave them grace, forgave them, and changed them. Think about the Scriptures that tell of those whom Jesus loved. Unlike the Pharisees, He loved sinners and tax collectors (Mark 2:15-17; Luke 19:1-9), a demoniac (Mark 5:1-20), a diseased woman (Mark 5:25-34), untouchable lepers (Luke 17:11-17), a Samaritan adulteress (John 4:1-30), and a doubting disciple (John 20:24-29). He even used a formerly demon-possessed woman to tell the disciples about His resurrection (Luke 8:2; John 20:1-2).

In many of these cases, Jesus loved those no one else would have readily loved—and who themselves might have felt unloved. How do you think they responded when Jesus offered love to them?

In your Bible, read the stories listed here. Then match the story with the character's reaction to Jesus' love.

_____ 1. Mark 5:1-20 (v. 18)   A. "I'll give half of my possessions to the poor."

_____ 2. Luke 19:1-9 (v. 8)   B. "My Lord and my God!"

_____ 3. John 4:1-30 (v. 29)   C. He begged Jesus to let him stay with Him.

_____ 4. John 20:24-29 (v. 28)   D. "Come, see a man who told me everything I ever did!"

Those touched by Jesus' love in these stories reacted strongly. The demoniac pleaded with Jesus, anxious to stay with Him. The Samaritan woman returned to a city that had rejected her and encouraged them to come meet Jesus. Zacchaeus offered to give half of his possessions to the poor and to repay in quadruple what he had stolen from others. Thomas simply worshiped Jesus.

What was your reaction to Jesus' love when you first met Him? What is your reaction to His love today?

Describe any ways that your response to Jesus' love is different today from the first time you met Him. If it's stronger today, thank God for showing His love to you. If it's not as strong, ask God's forgiveness. Thank Him for continuing to love you even when your love for Him sometimes wavers.

_____

_____

_____

In Christ, We Are Forgiven and Changed

Read the story of the adulteress in John 8:2-12.

This woman was caught in the very act of adultery. In fact, it's quite likely that one of her accusers had been the one with her. How else would she have been caught in the act? She couldn't deny her sin, nor could she blame someone else for her actions. She was, to state the case simply, guilty.

According to the law of her day, the penalty for adultery was stoning (Lev. 20:10; Deut. 22:23-24). So she not only bore the shame of her sin but also faced impending death by stoning. She could say or do nothing to change the situation. Her anguish must have been intense. Such is our situation, too, if we aren't wearing the helmet of salvation. Guilty and condemned before a holy God, we can do nothing on our own to stay the judgment of God.

For the woman in John 8, though, Jesus intervened. Challenging her accusers to confront their own sin first (v. 7), Jesus waited as, one by one, the accusers turned and walked away. He then forgave the woman of her sin and commanded her not to live in sin from that day forward.

Can you imagine her feelings when Jesus said, "Neither do I condemn you"? At one moment she was about to die; at the next, she was granted life. In an instant, Jesus transformed her from a condemned, guilty woman to a freed, forgiven one. Her accusers had dragged her to Jesus for judgment, but she walked away with Jesus as her Savior. What joy forgiveness brings!

In week 3, day 5 we studied Paul's testimony recorded in Acts 26:1-23. In other New Testament passages, Paul added details about his conversion. Record phrases that describe Paul's life prior to his meeting Christ.

Acts 9:1-2 _____

What God Does with Our Sins
- He removes them from us as far as the east is from the west (Ps. 103:12).
- He remembers them no more (Isa. 43:25).
- He sweeps them away like a cloud (Isa. 44:22).
- He casts them into the depth of the sea (Mic. 7:19).
- Ultimately He forgives us and cleanses us of all unrighteousness (1 John 1:9).

Acts 22:3-5 _____

Galatians 1:13-14 _____

Perhaps you wrote phrases such as "persecuted the church of God," "born a Jew," "zealous for God," and "lived as a strict Pharisee." Clearly, Paul was deeply committed to his Jewish faith—until Jesus encountered him on a road to Damascus. When Jesus saved Paul, He forgave him and changed Paul's entire life. Paul had been:

- spiritually lost, but Jesus found him and saved him;
- passionate for the Law, but now he lived in grace;
- furiously fighting against the church, but now he was one of the church;
- willingly a murderer, but he became a proclaimer of life;
- zealous in his Judaism, but now he became zealous for Christ;
- killing others for the cause of Judaism, but he was now willing to die for the cause of Christ.

Paul's story ought to give us all hope. I know a prisoner named Mike who first found his hope in that story. Mike had committed a serious crime and had been in prison for over 20 years when I met him. By that time, he was a Christian who preached the Word and discipled new believers in the prison yard. The change in his life, I am told, was drastic.

Loved. Forgiven. Changed. Those words define who we are in Christ. Wearing the helmet of salvation means believing this truth, even when the Enemy attacks us with false messages. Nothing Satan says to us can halt our advance when we know who we are in Christ.

Loved. Forgiven. Changed.

𖣘 DAILY IN THE WORD 𖣘
Ephesians 4:17-24

Paul continued his discourse on practical aspects of the Christian life, specifically speaking about the lifestyle transformation in the life of a Christian. He reminded his readers that they should no longer live the way they once lived. Instead, they were to live in a new way, described as taking off the old man and putting on the new man. The new man is "created according to God's likeness in righteousness and purity of the truth" (v. 24).

Darkness, hardness of heart, immorality, and impurity marked our lives prior to Christ. A drastic change took place, though, when we discovered that the truth is in Jesus. Now, the Holy Spirit renews our minds, and we learn to walk as a new person by putting on the armor of God through obedient Christian living.

APPLICATION
- Think about the person who told you about the truth of Jesus. If possible, write him or her a thank-you note.
- Thank God for the change He has produced in your life.

MEMORY VERSE FOR THIS WEEK
"Be kind and compassionate to one another, forgiving one another, just as God also forgave you in Christ." Ephesians 4:32

Answers to activity on page 95: 1. C; 2. A; 3. D; 4. B

day  *four*

WEARING THE HELMET DAILY

Think about what you do every day. You eat, drink, brush your teeth, and shower. You get dressed and go to work or you work at home. You eat again and sleep. Then the routine starts again the next morning. Sounds rather boring, doesn't it?

Yet all of these daily steps matter, don't they? If you don't eat and drink, you die. If you don't brush your teeth and shower, disease can set in or you'll lose all your friends. If you don't get dressed, you get arrested. If you don't work, you don't eat. And if you don't sleep, your body and mind succumb to exhaustion. Day-to-day steps that seem basic are actually critical for survival.

Likewise, we make daily choices that determine the effectiveness of our Christian living. Wearing the helmet of salvation means that we choose every day to walk in the joy of our salvation. But the Enemy works every day to rob us of that joy. In day 4 we will learn how to make the right daily choices while defeating the Enemy, who always targets the joy of our salvation.

We Are to Take Up Our Cross Daily

Have you ever read instructions for assembling something and the instructions were so unclear that you had no idea where to begin? Or rarer, the instructions were actually helpful? Sometimes it's just easier to hire somebody to assemble it for you.

When Jesus gave instructions and requirements for following Him, they were clear. Read Luke 9:23 below, and underline the three conditions that Jesus laid out for following Him.

Then He said to them all, "If anyone wants to come with Me, he must deny himself, take up his cross daily, and follow Me."

You most likely found these three expectations with ease: deny yourself, take up your cross daily, and follow Jesus. Jesus' words were quite clear, but understanding what He *meant* by them is most important.

To deny self means to reject a life built around self-interest, self-fulfillment, and self-glorification. It means to walk with Jesus regardless of the personal cost.

To take up our cross daily is to be willing to die for Jesus. Picture a condemned criminal who is forced to carry his own cross to his execution; however, in this case, the disciple of Jesus willingly takes up his cross. Such a deep commitment demands that we renew this pledge every day.

To follow Jesus means that we continually trust Him and obey His commands, walking in His footsteps as the disciple following the Master. Thus, wearing the helmet of salvation includes all three of these steps: saying no to self, accepting the cost of obedience, and following Christ *every* day.

Write these steps in your memory by jotting them down in the list in the margin. Then think about how contrary these steps are to the way the Enemy works. The following activity will help you.

Steps to Following Jesus:

1. _____

2. _____

3. _____

In your Bible, read each of these passages, and briefly compare Jesus' expectations with the Enemy's tactics.

1. Genesis 3:4-6—Jesus says, "Deny yourself," but the Enemy says,

"_____

_____ ."

2. Matthew 16:21-23—Jesus says, "Take up your cross," but the Enemy says,

"_____

_____ ."

3. Luke 4:5-7—Jesus says, "Follow me," but the Enemy says, "_____

_____

_____ ."

You see how differently the Enemy thinks? He wants us to indulge ourselves, never denying ourselves what we think we deserve. He doesn't want us to be willing to die (and he even used Peter to suggest that Jesus should not die). In the end, he wants us to follow him rather than God.

As we wear the helmet of salvation daily, we must choose to focus on God and reject the Enemy's tactics. It probably won't surprise you that we keep our focus on God by walking in truth and righteousness, standing firmly in our faith, telling others about God, and trusting the promises of His Word. We daily wear *God's* armor into the battle.

The Enemy Seeks to Lead Us Astray

Why do you suppose Jesus told us to take up His cross daily? One reason is that the Enemy attacks us every day. He aims his darts at us so that we will lose our joy and give the helmet of salvation little meaning. Let's return to the story of Simon Peter to help us think about how the Enemy attacks us.

Read Luke 22:31-34,54-62 in your Bible.

In this passage, Jesus warned Peter that Satan wanted to sift him like wheat (v. 31)— that he sought to shake him violently as a woman shakes wheat through a sieve to separate the chaff. This sifting would result in Peter's temporary fall. Look at the text again to see how Satan accomplished his task.

First, Peter was overconfident in his faith (v. 33). Peter surely believed his own words when he said that he would die for Jesus; in fact, he later defended Jesus in the garden of Gethsemane (Luke 22:47-51; John 18:10-11). Nevertheless, Peter denied Jesus three times before dawn the next morning.

Second, Peter denied Jesus by his actions and his words. The apostle warmed himself at the fire of Jesus' attackers (Luke 22:54-55), and he at least temporarily blended in with the crowd. Then, when he was directly confronted about his relationship with Jesus, he denied knowing Him (vv. 56-60). At this point, he was hardly denying self, taking up his cross, or following Jesus.

Here's the picture, at least in Peter's case: His overconfidence led to letting his guard down, resulting in his mingling with enemies of Jesus and denying Christ. The story is not over, of course, but Peter had failed. At least briefly, the Enemy had shaken Peter so violently that he denied the very Savior who had given him the helmet of salvation.

In each of the following, indicate how often you give in to the Enemy's tactics.

	Always	Sometimes	Never
1. I blend in with the crowd.	_____	_____	_____
2. I get overconfident in my faith.	_____	_____	_____
3. I deny Jesus by my actions.	_____	_____	_____
4. I mingle too long with people who drag me down.	_____	_____	_____
5. I fail to proclaim my commitment to Jesus when an opportunity arises.	_____	_____	_____
6. I let my guard down.	_____	_____	_____
7. My words or actions deny that I'm clothed with the helmet of salvation.	_____	_____	_____

Repentance Breaks the Enemy's Hold

Perhaps you remember Luke 22:61-62 from week 3, day 2: "Then the Lord turned and looked at Peter. So Peter remembered the word of the Lord, how He had said to him, 'Before the rooster crows today, you will deny Me three times.' And he went outside and wept bitterly." Immediately after Peter denied Jesus, the Lord looked straight at him, and Peter recalled the Lord's prophesy of his betrayal. Guilty and broken, he wept uncontrollably. Just weeks later, however, he preached on the day of Pentecost when thousands became believers (Acts 2).

Take note of this process because it's so similar to the course that we follow when the Enemy seeks to destroy the joy of our salvation. We sin, denying the Lord by our actions and word; but the Lord doesn't take His eyes off of us, and He doesn't allow us to forget His teachings. God graciously brings us to brokenness and repentance, restores the joy of our salvation, and uses us to teach others about the dangers of rebellion and the joy of return (Ps. 51:12-13).

Repentance is a non-negotiable component of this process. When I travel, I often request a Global Positioning System (GPS) in my rental car. This system amazingly maps my progress, tells me where I am and when to turn, and hollers at me when I miss a turn. Even with a GPS, I still sometimes miss a turn, and the system says in a computerized voice, "When possible, make a legal U-turn!" That's how repentance works—God graciously leads us to make a U-turn away from our sin and back to Him. The Enemy loses when we've made that turn.

Wearing the helmet of salvation means experiencing the joy of turning to Christ daily, following Him, and returning to Him in repentance when we fail. Describe a time when the Enemy temporarily robbed you of your joy—but God intervened and restored your joy.

_____

_____

_____

Have you lost your joy? Is there some sin from which you need to repent?

DAILY IN THE WORD
Ephesians 4:25-32

Today's reading shows us what happens when we take off the "old man" and put on the "new man." Paul began by saying, "you put away lying," (v. 25) and he told the Ephesians to speak truth to their neighbors. He allowed for anger, but without letting "the sun go down on your anger" (v. 26). The thief "must no longer steal" but rather "must do honest work with his own hands" (v. 28). Talk should not be "rotten talk," but instead it should be words only for "the building up of someone in need" (v. 29). The Ephesians were to rid their lives of "bitterness, anger and wrath, insult and slander" (v. 31) and to be full of compassion for one another instead. They were to be careful not to give the Devil an open door, and they were not to grieve the Holy Spirit.

Texts like these not only call us away from sinful behavior, but they also direct us to live lives that are holy and pleasing to God.

APPLICATION
- Evaluate your life—if it doesn't show a change since you met Christ, something isn't right. Talk to your pastor or group leader.
- Confess to God any bitterness or anger in your life.

MEMORY VERSE FOR THIS WEEK
"Be kind and compassionate to one another, forgiving one another, just as God also forgave you in Christ." Ephesians 4:32

day *five*

LIVING IN HOPE

From the garden of Eden until today, the Enemy has strategized to attack the people of God. If we were to reduce the Enemy's strategies to two simple tactics, they would be these: he wants us to mess up or give up. We mess up when we fall into sin. We give up when discouragement sets in and the battle wears us out.

Discouragement can present problems for believers. Maybe you know a believer who has given much for Christ, only to be hurt by the sins of others. Or perhaps you've seen Christians whose faith weakened when God didn't answer their prayers as they wished. Or, perhaps you're in the midst of discouragement even while you study this material. The Enemy wants to rob us of our hope because he knows that discouraged Christians are defeated Christians.

In 1 Thessalonians 5:8 Paul used the image of a helmet to describe the "hope of salvation." Our goal today is to see how wearing the helmet of salvation gives us hope when discouragement sets in.

Discouragement Happens Even to God's People

When I first became a believer, I thought the Christian life would be filled with complete joy and excitement. Never again would I have any feelings of discouragement—or so I thought. Before long (like perhaps about one day), I found myself discouraged because some unbelieving friends didn't want to hear the gospel. I just couldn't understand why everyone wouldn't want what I had gained through Christ, and I grew increasingly disappointed as more and more friends chose to reject the good news.

I learned later that the Bible is filled with stories of good people who sometimes faced times of discouragement. Use this activity to review some of them.

> **Match the biblical characters below with the corresponding statement that might best describe their discouragement.**
>
> 1. ＿＿ Elijah (1 Kings 19:9-14) A. "Everyone ridicules me."
>
> 2. ＿＿ Job (Job 3:1-7) B. "We don't understand what has happened. We're confused in our faith."
>
> 3. ＿＿ Jeremiah (Jer. 20:7-10) C. "I'm the only faithful one left."
>
> 4. ＿＿ Disciples on the road to Emmaus (Luke 24:13-35) D. "With all the pain I now face, I wish I had never been born."

The causes of discouragement for these biblical characters were numerous. Elijah believed he was the "only" faithful person left and that loneliness made him vulnerable to attack. Job simply could not understand why he was born. Jeremiah tired of preaching with no positive response from the people.

Wearing the helmet of salvation gives us hope when discouragement sets in.

The disciples on the road to Emmaus had been on an emotional roller coaster. Jesus had died and been buried, but now they had heard that He was alive again—though they had not yet seen Him. Their hopes had been dashed when Jesus died, and they weren't sure what to do with the rumors of His resurrection. The disciples' confusion and questions led to discouragement.

Faith didn't automatically eliminate discouragement for these followers of God. In some cases—like Jeremiah's and Job's—discouragement occurred while they were walking obediently with God. Being faithful today doesn't guarantee that we won't be discouraged tomorrow.

Most of the time, discouragement occurs when life doesn't go as we expected. Have you ever felt as if you were fighting the battle alone, like Elijah? Have you endured such tragedies in your life that you wished you had not been born, as in Job's case? Have you ever grown weary of teaching truth when everyone rejected your message, like Jeremiah? Maybe you have ridden the emotional roller coaster like the disciples on the road to Emmaus.

Write in the margin what you believe to be the source of your discouragement. Discouraged warriors are seldom effective warriors in spiritual battles. Indeed, the Enemy rejoices when we lose our joy. Few soldiers win battles when they no longer have a will to fight.

Think again about faithful believers like Job and the disciples on the Emmaus Road. Why do you think God didn't immediately free these followers from their discouragement?

_____

_____

Since God chose to bless Job after a period of time (Job 42:10), why did He wait? Jesus could have quickly stopped the confused thinking of the men on the road to Emmaus. All He would have had to do was to identify Himself. Yet He chose to wait for the men to realize that He was the risen Christ. Waiting on God is one of the Christian's most challenging tasks. In each case, God is preparing His warriors for battles yet to come by building their faith—their hope—on what has not been seen. In short, for faithful followers the result is more faith!

Ask God to give you strength to trust Him and follow Him in spite of your discouragement.

We Hope in the Return of Christ

Paul wrote in 1 Thessalonians 5:8, "Since we are of the day, we must be sober and put the armor of faith and love on our chests, and put on a helmet of the hope of salvation." In 1 Thessalonians 4:13–5:11, Paul reminded his readers of the suddenness of Jesus' return and challenged them to be ready for His coming.

Others would be unprepared, ignoring the possibility of His coming as if they were sleeping in the darkness (5:1-7). The Thessalonian believers, though, were to be on guard, filled with spiritual steadiness ("sober"). They were to walk in faith and love, symbolized here by wearing a breastplate. In that sense, wearing the breastplate of righteousness in Ephesians 6 includes exhibiting faith and love.

POSSIBLE CAUSES OF DISCOURAGEMENT
- Loneliness
- Broken relationships
- Seemingly unanswered prayer
- Recurrent sin
- Apparently unfruitful Christian service
- Confusion about God's will

My cause: _____

_____

_____

Their helmet, then, was a helmet of the "hope of salvation." In this case, the "hope of salvation" refers to the hope that the Thessalonians had in the second coming of Christ. Because they believed and trusted that Christ would return for them, the hope of that event challenged them to be faithful as they waited. The hope of a promised future event changed the way they lived in the present.

More In-Depth Study
Using a Bible dictionary and a modern dictionary, compare and contrast the different understandings of *hope*. Why is Christian hope different from the world's hope?

Our Hope Helps Us Win Today's Battles
Not long after I became a believer, the movie "A Thief in the Night" released. This movie told fictional stories of lives affected when Jesus snatched His children away in the rapture. Looking back, I think the movie had a gripping story. Few people in our church—including me—left unchanged after watching this vivid depiction of Christ's return.

I wish I could say that those changes stuck around permanently. Some of us witnessed more faithfully, but only for a few weeks. We tried to read the Bible more consistently, just in case Jesus came back soon—but that habit soon declined. Repentance from our besetting sins was sometimes only temporary. In the end, our fear of Christ's return failed to affect our daily living for any length of time.

Paul expected more from the Thessalonians. The truth of Christ's impending return inspired them to guard against wrong and to press on with living in the light. The hope of their salvation was not an uncertain hope; rather, they were to believe with such certainty in the coming of Christ that they would always be ready and prepared to welcome Him. They were to be on deployment when He came.

Do you hope with certainty that Jesus is going to return? If so, does that confident hope change the way you live? Do you overcome discouragement because your hope in Christ is real? Wearing the helmet of salvation, we can live in victory.

Suppose you knew for certain that Christ were going to return one week from today. List three ways your life would likely change in preparation for His return. Then circle one way you will work on beginning today.

1. _____

2. _____

3. _____

A Review: Wearing the Full Armor of God
Let's look again at the interconnected nature of the armor of God. We can't wear the helmet of salvation apart from Jesus, who is truth and righteousness. Nor would we know about our need for salvation or God's provision without the truth of God's Word. Now that we do know His grace, our natural response should be to tell others about Him and the peace He offers.

To be prepared for Christ's coming we need to live in truth, walk in righteousness, and stand firmly in faith. At peace with God and others, we will be found armed and deployed at His return.

DAILY IN THE WORD
Ephesians 5:1-5

These verses summarize the previous section. Those who put on the "new man" are to give evidence of their internal change. They should imitate God, just as children imitate their parents. Their motive for imitating Him is a response to the deep love the Messiah has for His children. He showed His love through His death, "a sacrificial and fragrant offering to God" (v. 2). The Father was pleased with that offering. As He loved us, so we are to love each other.

Moreover, He adopted us as His own, made us His children, and expects us to walk in His footsteps. As God's children, we must reject sexual immorality, greed, and unholy speech. Although not an exhaustive list, these sins easily lure us. Those whose lifestyles reflect such deeds have no inheritance in God's eternal kingdom.

APPLICATION
- Determine a specific step you will take today to imitate God.
- As God's dearly loved child, plan to give a sacrificial gift to your local church this week.

MEMORY VERSE FOR THIS WEEK
"Be kind and compassionate to one another, forgiving one another, just as God also forgave you in Christ." Ephesians 4:32

Answers to activity on page 102: 1. C; 2. D; 3. A; 4. B

---

1. John Kramp, *Out of Their Faces and into Their Shoes* (Nashville: Broadman and Holman, 1997), 1-16.
2. Wayne Grudem, *Systematic Theology* (Grand Rapids: Zondervan, 1994), 575.

The Sword of the Spirit

REVIEWING THE FULL ARMOR OF GOD

Belt of _____
- Know Jesus.
- Know His Word.
- Live the Word.

Breastplate of _____
- Live like Jesus.
- Make right choices.
- Resist temptation.

Feet Sandaled with the Gospel of _____
- Stand ready in faith.
- Be at peace with God.
- Be at peace with others.
- Share your faith.

Shield of _____
- Know and live the Word of God.
- Act on your faith.
- Resist worry, fear, and doubt.
- Trust the promises of God.

Helmet of _____
- Understand who you were prior to salvation, and appreciate God's grace.
- Meditate on, and marvel at God's love and holiness shown in the cross.
- Live in the assurance of Christ's return.

The Millers have adjusted to their move across the country and are recovering bit by bit from the death of Ann's father. In fact, life has settled into a busy but consistent routine. In addition to Sunday worship, every Sunday night the family attends the small group Bible studies organized by their church's discipleship ministry. Ed and Ann are in the adult group, Al has plugged in with young adults, and Reba loves the high-school study.

Lately though, Ed and Ann have been considering dropping out of their group. They just "haven't been getting anything out of the study," as Ed said. They've done their homework every week, yet it seems as though they're just going through the motions without real life change. Surely they can study their Bibles just as well on their own.

How would you advise Ed and Ann? What do you think the Enemy is saying to them? What might be wrong with their conclusion? Isn't studying the Bible individually as good as studying it in a group or with a study book? What effect would their dropping out have on Al and Reba? In week 6, we'll look at the importance of studying the Word of God both individually and with other believers. The sword of the Spirit is indeed a powerful and essential weapon in our spiritual arsenal.

day *one*

BELIEVING IN THE POWER OF THE WORD

I have kept every positive note or card that I've received in over 25 years of ministry. (I toss the negative ones, and I've received some of those, too!) Keeping these memories for more than two decades may seem a bit strange, but I enjoy reading them when life gets tough.

One is especially important to me. When I resigned from my first church, one child whom I had baptized was especially grieved. She wrote me a good-bye note; however, she didn't spell well, and her card said: "Dear Brother Chuck, I wish you didn't have to live. I love you." It took me a few minutes to figure out that she had

misspelled "leave," but I finally got it. She didn't want her pastor—the only pastor she had ever known—to go.

Despite the spelling error, her words remain precious to me to this day. Words really do have power, especially those words from affirming human beings. How much more powerful are the words God inspired, protected, and gave to us as His Word? Day 1 will remind us about the power of God's Word, and the remaining days will demonstrate how to study His Word in depth.

The Word Teaches Us Who God Is

Imagine a jet fighter dropping a bomb from the sky or a warship launching a missile miles from the intended target. These pictures describe contemporary warfare, not spiritual warfare. The Devil is a face-to-face attacker. In fact, the word translated "sword" in Ephesians 6:17 is the word used for the short sword that a Roman soldier carried for close combat. He used this sword when he stood face-to-face with an enemy combatant. We need the sword of the Spirit to defend ourselves in these battles with the Enemy.

The sword of the Spirit is "the most conspicuously offensive weapon" in all of the armor that God gives us.[1] In week 1, we learned that the Word of God is perfect, trustworthy, right, radiant, pure, reliable, and rewarding (Ps. 19:7-11). This perfect sword of the Spirit shows us who God is and reminds us that He is *much greater* than the Enemy.

Read each of the following verses that compare the Devil and God. Thank God for who He is as you fill in the blanks.

Satan is ...   but God ...

1. a destroyer (Rev. 9:11)   is the _____
                                     (Gen. 1:1).

2. limited by God (Job 1:12)   is _____
                                     (Gen. 17:1).

3. the father of lies (John 8:44)   is _____
                                     (John 14:6).

4. a murderer (John 8:44)   is _____
                                     (1 John 4:8).

5. evil (Matt. 6:13)   is _____ (Jer. 23:6).

6. our accuser (Rev. 12:10)   is our _____
                                 (1 John 2:1).

7. the tempter (Matt. 4:3)   always provides a way out of
                                 _____ (1 Cor. 10:13).

The Word teaches that God is creator, almighty, truth, love, and righteousness. Jesus is our advocate with the Father, who always provides a way out of temptation. When we know these truths about God as revealed in the Word, we are equipped to stand against the Enemy who gets in our face. The Word reminds us that God will judge the Enemy (Rev. 20:1-3).

What power exists in the Word of God! But living in obedience takes more than just reading and believing the Word; it also takes trusting the Spirit to convict us and empower us (John 16:7-10; Acts 1:8). Note in Acts 1–3 the difference between scared believers and active witnesses, simply because of the indwelling power of the Spirit. Read the Word, and don't ignore the Spirit by depending on yourself instead of God.

The Word Teaches Us That God Is Sovereign over the Enemy

We are in a real battle against a real Enemy, but the Enemy has *never* been outside of God's control. Even when he is face-to-face against us, he is still on God's leash. If this truth is difficult for you to accept, think about biblical examples.

Satan attacked Job, but he could go only as far as God allowed him (Job 1:6-12). In one of Zechariah's visions, God would not allow the accuser to condemn Joshua the high priest (Zech. 3:1-5). The demons exorcised from a demoniac in the Gerasenes could go only where Jesus permitted them (Luke 8:32). Satan had to ask permission from God to attack Peter (Luke 22:31). Paul struggled with a thorn in the flesh that he called a "messenger of Satan," but God determined whether the thorn would be removed (2 Cor. 12:7-10).

How does this truth help us when we're under attack? First, God always has a greater purpose for us when He allows the Enemy to attack us. He uses battles to conform us to the image of Christ (Rom. 8:29), and that conforming happens as warfare forces us to depend on God for our strength.

Second, the Enemy doesn't strike us with random attacks. Although he may not realize it, his attacks somehow fit into God's sovereign plan. What the Enemy means for evil, God turns to good (Gen. 50:19-20).

Third, our victory in the battle depends on God's accomplishing His will rather than on our strength to fight. We are still commanded to put on the armor; therefore, both our preparation for and response to attack are important. The Word gives us this powerful, good news: God gains the victory.

The Word Teaches Us That God Will Bind the Enemy

Maybe you like to read good mystery novels. The fun of reading mysteries is trying to figure out the end of the story before you get there. Sometimes you get it right, but often you're surprised—and that's the author's goal.

God had no such goal when He inspired the Word. He had no intention of leaving us guessing about the Enemy's future: he will be bound and thrown into the lake of fire (Rev. 20:1-3,7-10). God's always been in control of the Enemy.

Even when he is face-to-face against us, the Enemy is still on God's leash.

At what point would the Devil have been completely unbound? He was not able to keep Jesus from His crucifixion, death, and resurrection which provided our salvation. From his judgment in the garden of Eden to his imprisonment in the end, Satan has been, is being, and will be bound.

Now, put all of these truths together. God is greater than the Enemy. We find all of these truths in the Word of God, which Paul calls the sword of the Spirit. This sword is indeed powerful, and with its truths in mind, we should be willing to march forward in Christian obedience.

Mark any of the following statements that reflect your thoughts.

❏ If I really believed the truths of this lesson, I would be more willing to take risks for God.
❏ I want to believe these truths, but I struggle with believing Satan is under God's control.
❏ I've learned some truths that will encourage and strengthen me in my spiritual battles.
❏ I'm reading the Word consistently, and I am ready each day to be equipped and deployed.

DAILY IN THE WORD
Ephesians 5:6-14

As Paul continued the practical portion of his book, he called the Ephesians to live in obedience and guard themselves against disobedience. Because they were now "children of light," they were to walk that way (v. 8). Their lives should be characterized by goodness, righteousness, and truth: everything pleasing to the Lord.

Lives marked by darkness are full of corruption, depravity, and sin. The Ephesians were not to partner in that lifestyle. The works of darkness are fruitless, meaning they are not what God desires. Darkness provides cover for a shameful lifestyle, but the light of Christians exposes the darkness for what it is.

As Christians, we are neither to live like the world nor be so separate from the world that we can't influence it. The light of Christ in us can transform those who are sleeping in the darkness.

APPLICATION
- Turn from any area of darkness in your life.
- Intentionally reach out to and do a good deed for a nonbeliever this week. Be "light" in someone's life.

MEMORY VERSE FOR THIS WEEK
"You were once darkness, but now you are light in the Lord. Walk as children of light." Ephesians 5:8

day **two**

RECOGNIZING THE ENEMY'S STRATEGIES

Just before the end of World War II, the United States decided to drop the first atomic bomb used in warfare. The decision to do so was difficult, as no one could be absolutely certain how many lives would be lost. To this day, scholars debate the ethics of unleashing a bomb that killed hundreds of thousands of civilians. The United States had incredible power at its disposal and chose to use it.

Day 1 focused on the power of God's Word, the sword of the Spirit. The Word is "inspired by God and is profitable for teaching, for rebuking, for correcting, for training in righteousness, so that the man of God may be complete, equipped for every good work" (2 Tim. 3:16-17). The Enemy loses the victory when we quote Scripture, such is its power. Yet, many believers fail to read and follow the Word consistently, much less memorize significant verses. We often choose not to use the power at hand.

Do you know how the Enemy works to keep us from reading and memorizing the Word? Perhaps you'll see how he works in your life in this area as you study this lesson. Let's begin with a time of reflection.

> **Circle any of the following phrases that describe why you may struggle with reading the Word consistently.**

I'm too busy.	I'm not trained on how to use the Bible.
I don't understand the words.	I get frustrated trying to interpret it.
It makes me feel guilty.	I don't know where to start.
I don't really believe the Bible is the Word of God.	I've tried to read it before, but it didn't help me live more faithfully.

The Enemy loses the victory when we quote Scripture.

The Enemy Leads Us to Doubt God's Character and His Word

We've already seen that the strategy of casting doubt isn't new. The serpent challenged God's Word in the garden of Eden (Gen. 3:1-5). If God's Word isn't accurate or can't be trusted, we have no legitimate authority on which to base our Christian lives. We learned in week 1 that the Word claims to be truth (Num. 23:19; Ps. 19:7; 119:86; Prov. 30:5; 2 Tim. 3:16), but the Enemy doesn't want us to accept those claims.

The nature of God rests as the foundation of this discussion. Because God "inspired" Scripture (2 Tim. 3:16), studying His character and the nature of His words will help us understand the truth of Scripture. The activity will guide you.

Read each of the verses below, and complete the statement about ⁀'s words.

⁀⁀:19	God isn't a man who _____.
⁀ ⁀amuel 7:28	God's words are _____.
John 17:17	God's word is _____.
Titus 1:2	God can't _____.
Hebrews 6:18	It's impossible for God to _____.

The argument is simple but clearly scriptural. God doesn't lie; His words are truth. If He inspired the words of Scripture, we can trust that Scripture is entirely true and that the Enemy is entirely wrong when he leads us to doubt the Word.

The Enemy Wants to Substitute Religion for Knowing the Word

Read the words Jesus spoke to the Sadducees, religious leaders in His day. Underline any words implying that the Enemy was at work in this situation.

Are you not deceived because you don't know the Scriptures or the power of God? ... You are badly deceived (Mark 12:24,27).

Jesus reminded these religious leaders that they didn't even know their own Scriptures. Twice Jesus told the Sadducees that they were deceived, suggesting the Enemy's hand in their lives. What led Jesus to speak these words?

The Sadducees didn't believe in a resurrection, yet they asked Jesus a question about the resurrection (see Mark 12:18-27). "If a man marries a woman and dies," they said, "Moses told us that his brother should marry her and produce children with her for his deceased brother's sake. But what if a family of seven brothers all died, each having married this woman as required. Whose wife would she be in the resurrection?" The Sadducees may have asked this preposterous question simply to ridicule Jesus' belief in an afterlife.

Whatever their reason, Jesus took the discussion to a higher level. Moses' teaching to which the Sadducees referred didn't even mention the afterlife and wasn't intended to give direction about eternal relationships. (See Deut. 25:5-10.) Moreover, Jesus reminded them that while they were debating "the dead being raised" (Mark 12:26), they had missed the point from their own Scriptures. God isn't the God of the dead but of the living. God is a present-tense God. According to Jesus, the Sadducees didn't know His Word.

I recently attended an upbeat, energetic church service designed to reach the younger generation. The loud music was still reverent, and the crowd seemed to enjoy the worship. A great communicator, the pastor forcefully preached while holding my attention through humor and illustrations. The problem was that he used very little of the Bible, and (I thought) what he did use he interpreted wrongly and applied poorly. In the end, he gave a religious talk that lacked biblical support.

Serving as leaders and teachers in the church without really knowing God's Word is dangerous. If we can lead the church without knowing the Word, why take

God is a present-tense God.

111

time to read, know, and memorize it now? When we lead without knowing the Word, we risk misleading people—and the Enemy delights in that possibility.

Place an "x" on the line near the description that best indicates your current Bible knowledge.

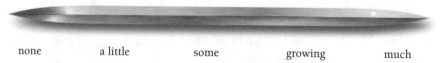

none   a little   some   growing   much

The Enemy Wants Us to Listen to Voices Other than God's

God had given Adam His mandate forbidding them to eat from the tree of the knowledge of good and evil (Gen. 2:16-17). Apparently, Adam told Eve about God's instructions sometime before the serpent spoke to Eve. But when that serpent spoke, they were faced with a decision: to whose voice would they listen? Their choice proved fatal.

That wouldn't be the last time God's people would need to make a choice between opposing voices. Job faced a choice between the voices of his friends and God's voice (Job 4–42). The psalmist understood that happiness comes by rejecting the advice of the wicked and instead delighting in the instruction of the Lord (Ps. 1:1-2). The exiled Hebrews in Babylon heard their false prophets proclaim a message different from that of Jeremiah, God's prophet (Jer. 29). Malachi prophesied against the priests of Israel, but they chose which instruction to follow (Mal. 2:1-9).

Even Jesus faced the battle of choosing which voice to follow. The Enemy offered Him the kingdoms of the world on the mount of temptation (Matt. 4:8-9), and Jesus chose to reject the Enemy's voice to follow the Father's call (Matt. 4:10; 26:39). Later, He again chose the Father's will when He struggled in His humanity in the garden of Gethsemane. "Not My will, but Yours, be done" (Luke 22:42) was His affirmation that He would listen to the Father's voice above any others.

Of course, we face choices. Think about some other voices that beckon us:

- the media that often reject Christian values
- political correctness that insists our belief in Jesus as the only way to heaven is arrogant
- fictional religious novels that influence our doctrine
- a judicial system that at times legislates in opposition to Christian morals
- a culture that proclaims as acceptable many actions and attitudes the Bible condemns
- popular church leaders who preach that the Christian life should lead to prosperity, health, and happiness
- others: _____

_____

The Enemy speaks loudly through these voices, and the options he offers are usually inviting. Sometimes it's easier to listen to these voices than to invest in reading and knowing God's Word. To be certain, it pleases the Devil when we ignore the sword of the Spirit that so threatens him. Decide now that you will read the Word of God and not be guided by the other voices.

It pleases the Devil when we ignore the sword of the Spirit.

🌿 DAILY IN THE WORD 🌿
Ephesians 5:15-21

In today's reading Paul continued to call for godliness by encouraging his readers to pay careful attention to the way they walked. They were to live with a sense of watchfulness and urgency, not missing any opportunities to do good in an evil world. Their goal was to walk "not as unwise people but as wise" (v. 15).

Moreover, the believers were to be continually filled and led by the Holy Spirit—and only by Him. The Holy Spirit led believers to express joy in singing, offering thanksgiving, and submitting to one another. This kind of submission is biblical love for others, characterized by self-denial, humility, and respect for brothers and sisters in Christ. When believers mutually submit to one another, we are best prepared to work together as the people of God.

APPLICATION
- Be alert to opportunities to do good in an evil world.
- If your ego hinders the mutual submission Paul calls for in this text, turn from your pride and humble yourself before the Lord.

MEMORY VERSE FOR THIS WEEK
"You were once darkness, but now you are light in the Lord. Walk as children of light." Ephesians 5:8

day *three*

COUNTERING THE ENEMY'S STRATEGIES

Keith is the offensive coordinator for the football team at a local Christian high school. His job is to challenge and guide his team to move the football past the opposing defensive players. That task might sound simple, but Keith spends hours planning his strategy.

At the same time, he struggles with reading and focusing on God's Word. Keith is a good strategist at football, but he has no strategy for reading the Word. Although he believes he should read the Bible, he seldom gets past the first few chapters of one of the books of the Bible.

As we learned in day 2, the Enemy has strategies to keep us from reading the Word of God. We shouldn't be surprised that the Enemy has specific strategies aimed against us; Paul told us to put on the armor of God in order to stand against his schemes (Eph. 6:11). The Devil's strategies sometimes attack us head-on, but more often he works subtly and slyly to catch us with our guard down. He is unlikely to say to us, "Hey, don't read the Word anymore," but he *is* likely to raise doubts that the Word is trustworthy.

The Enemy works to keep us from reading the Word; we must intentionally and consistently choose to read it. If we want to counter the Enemy's opposing strategies, we need a strategy as well. In day 3 we'll learn some simple ways to read the Word of God. While this lesson deals less directly with spiritual warfare, it will help us develop a reading strategy that counters the Enemy's subtle plans.

Develop a Reading and Study Plan

This guideline may seem elementary, but time management produces faithful Bible study. Not only does the Enemy fight against our reading the Word, but also we tend to push Bible study aside when we have so many other activities to do. Consider these ways to plan your reading and study.

Read through the Bible in a year. Did you know that you can finish the Bible in less than a year by reading four chapters each day? Bible reading is not necessarily Bible study, but it does provide light for study by giving us the entire scope of the Word of God. Many people can read the Bible in a year by devoting 30 or so minutes each day. I am currently following a plan that guides me to read through an Old Testament and New Testament book at the same time. As I write, I have already completed Genesis, Exodus, Leviticus, Job, Matthew, and most of Mark. Each day I know exactly what the reading plan requires, and I waste no time trying to figure out what to read.

Read through one book at a time. You've been following this process if you've been reading the Book of Ephesians each day. This process takes longer and often doesn't lead to completing the entire Bible in a single year, but reading in this way helps you see central themes and major teachings in a book, an important facet of Bible study. If reading Ephesians is your first attempt at reading an entire book, I recommend that you follow this study with one of the first three Gospels (Matthew, Mark, or Luke). You will read the inspiring stories of Jesus' life, and you will also see just how powerfully Jesus defeated the demonic forces He faced.

Do a doctrinal/topical study. Because we believe that the Scriptures are God's inspired Word to us, we must find our doctrine in the Bible. A Bible concordance lists by topic all of the Scriptures that contain a certain word. For example, you might take a look at the teachings about prayer, some of which are included in the activity below. We'll review some other texts next week.

Read each of the following Scriptures, and draw a line to its teaching about prayer. Check any teaching that is new or has new meaning to you at this stage in your Christian walk.

1. Isaiah 59:1-2   A. Prayer is not for show.

2. Matthew 6:5-8   B. Prayers of a righteous person make a difference.

3. 1 Thessalonians 5:17   C. Unhealthy relationships hinder prayers.

4. James 5:16   D. Believers are to live in a spirit of prayer.

5. 1 Peter 3:7   E. Sin builds barriers between us and God.

Choose a Bible character to study. You can probably tell from this study that I love the story of Simon Peter. His story fascinates me because he was a study in contrasts. He was willing to take risks for Jesus—like walking on water (Matt. 14:22-33), but he also suffered from a lack of faith. He fought for Jesus in the garden (John 18:10-11), but moments later refused to speak for Him in the camp of Jesus' enemies (John 18:15-18). After Christ's ascension, Peter preached the gospel at Pentecost (Acts 2:14-36).

Peter was a momentary failure who became a leader in the early church. Many times I return to read Peter's story because he was so remarkably human. When I wonder why God would dare use me in His church, Peter's story gives me hope.

Other character studies that have been helpful to me are the stories of Jacob (Gen. 25:19–50:3), Joshua (Ex. 17:8-13; 32:17; Num. 13:30–14:38; 27:15-23; Deut. 31:14-15,23; Joshua 1–24), Samson (Judges 13–16), David (1 Sam. 16– 2 Sam. 24; 1 Kings 1–2; 1 Chron. 11–29), and Andrew (Mark 1:16-18; John 1:35-42; 6:8; 12:20-22). Perhaps one of these studies will give you guidance and strength if you include it in your Bible reading plan.

Which study method most interests you?

❑ read the Bible in a year
❑ read one book at a time
❑ complete a doctrinal/topical study
❑ choose a Bible character to study

Do you think you will use this plan in the near future? ❑ yes ❑ no
If so, explain your plan, including how you will start.

_____

_____

Develop a Learning Plan

At first glance, this heading might seem to duplicate the previous one ("Develop a Reading and Study Plan"). In some ways, a learning plan and a reading and study plan are alike. You can't learn the Bible without reading and studying it! When we have a specific plan to reinforce and learn the Scriptures in-depth, the plan strengthens our reading of the Word.

I struggled for many years trying to develop a workable, effective Bible study plan that resulted in my learning the Word. I don't claim to have a perfect plan, and I wouldn't want to suggest that this method is the best one, but here is the strategy that helps me stay faithful to my learning plan.

1. **Follow a reading plan.** I have struggled most with obedience in Bible reading when I did not know the direction of my reading each day. Generally, my primary plan is to read through the Scriptures in a year. Others may prefer a book-by-book study, while some of you are given reading instructions from the Bible study group you attend regularly.

2. **Always pray before reading.** Ask the Holy Spirit to guide you in understanding and applying God's Word.

3. **Use a good study Bible.** The notes that accompany the text are not the inspired Word of God, but they can help us understand the Word. A good study Bible is worth the monetary investment.

4. **Don't be afraid to utilize good commentaries.** Again, commentaries are not inspired, but they are good resources to understand the background and the contexts of scriptural texts. One set including the 66 individual books will help you gain confidence in interpreting Scripture.

5. **As you read, be alert to verses to memorize.** I'm always more faithful to memorize a verse that arises out of my personal Bible study.

6. **Using good principles of interpretation (see week 1, day 3), look for truths, insights, and examples to guide you in Christian living. Find a workable method for recording these teachings.** My strategy is to highlight the passages with a Bible highlighter, and then write personal notes and applications in the margin. You may prefer to use a journal to record your reflections each day.

7. **Make any changes or commitments that the Scriptures require each day.** Reading the Word without being obedient to its teachings stops short of the Bible's purpose. In fact, the Enemy wins when we are disobedient. Consider making a specific list of action steps to take based on each day's readings (as I am helping you to do as you read Ephesians). Empowered by the Spirit, you'll change over time.

Join a Bible Study Group

Most likely, you are studying this material as part of a group—which is a great way to study the Scriptures. Studying the Bible in a group has several advantages. First, group study allows us to learn from each other. We might individually decide what the Bible teaches, but a group setting allows us to test our conclusions. We're more likely to reach the right conclusions when others give their input as well. Second, group study holds us accountable to our personal study. Other members of the group can push us to make sure that we're consistently reading God's Word. Third, the group with whom we study can minister to us in times of need. Group members sometimes become our closest friends and prayer partners. They are there to support us when we face spiritual battles.

Your church probably has other small-group study opportunities for when you complete this study. If you are not attending a Sunday School class or other small group, decide now to join a class. Maybe there are other discipleship group studies that you can join. The Enemy will not be pleased when you decide to study God's Word with other believers.

I have provided you with multiple strategies to read the Word so that you can take up the sword of the Spirit. Your task now is simply to do it in God's strength. Family or job responsibilities are not reasonable barriers. God gives us the time we need to accomplish His will, or He wouldn't ask us to do it. The question is more, "Where are your priorities?"

God gives us the time we need to accomplish His will, or He wouldn't ask us to do it.

What is the biggest obstacle you face to effective Bible study?

❏ time ❏ cost ❏ effort ❏ interest ❏ other _____

What is your plan to overcome that obstacle?

_____

❧❧ DAILY IN THE WORD ❧❧
Ephesians 5:22-24

This section begins what is known as the "house codes" that give guidance for relationships in the home. These verses call wives to live in submission to their husbands and husbands to love their wives. However, submission does not suggest forced obedience or mindless following. Instead, wives are to submit "as to the Lord"; that is, a wife should submit to her husband out of devotion to the Lord.

Paul teaches that a wife's submission maintains the structure God has established in the family unit. The husband is the "head of the wife as also Christ is head of the church" (v. 23), indicating that the husband is to lead his wife as Christ leads the church. That leadership assumes humility and godliness in the leader. A husband's love for his wife will make his heart tender toward her. His self-giving love for his wife strengthens and guides her. Submission to that kind of love should not be difficult.

APPLICATION
- If you are married, make deliberate choices to strengthen your marriage. Love each other with Christ's love.
- Begin today to pray every day for your spouse and, when possible, with your spouse.

MEMORY VERSE FOR THIS WEEK
"You were once darkness, but now you are light in the Lord. Walk as children of light." Ephesians 5:8

Answers to activity on page 114: 1. E; 2. A; 3. D; 4. B; 5. C

day *four*

OVERCOMING THE ENEMY'S LIES
⚜⚜⚜⚜⚜⚜⚜⚜⚜⚜⚜⚜⚜⚜⚜⚜⚜⚜⚜⚜⚜⚜⚜⚜⚜⚜⚜⚜

About six months after his powerful conversion, Patrick's friends invited him to a party for all of their college buddies. Patrick knew there would be drinking at the party, but he was nervously convinced that he could withstand temptation. After all, he was a Christian now.

You might imagine the rest of the story. The pressure for this young Christian was too much when his friends urged him to drink. "One drink won't hurt," he convinced himself. But one drink became two, and two became three, and many then led to drunkenness. It was as if things had never changed for Patrick.

That next week, Patrick became convinced that God wouldn't forgive him for his wrongdoing. He had committed himself to follow Christ, but he had chosen his friends over obedience. Why would God ever forgive him? Defeated and discouraged, Patrick even found himself doubting his Christian conversion.

In times of disobedience, have you doubted your salvation? If so, what was the outcome? If not, what would you do if you were in Patrick's shoes? What would help Patrick the most? Would you turn to the Scriptures for direction?

One aspect of rightly using the sword of the Spirit is to know God's Word well enough to respond biblically to the Enemy's lies (which is another reason that he doesn't want us to read the Word). In day 4 we'll learn to counter three of the lies.

"God Won't Forgive You."

Patrick heard this lie first, followed quickly by doubts about his salvation. The Enemy knew that if he could discourage Patrick enough, this young believer would no longer be an effective witness for Christ. So he targeted Patrick, and the Enemy's arrows hit their mark.

One way to help Patrick is to remind him of the kinds of people God forgives. This activity will give you examples that you can share with others in Patrick's situation.

Read each of the following stories, and then describe the person God forgives.

1. Mark 5:25-34 _____

_____

2. Luke 7:36-50 _____

_____

3. Luke 8:1-2 _____

_____

4. Luke 19:1-10 _____

_____

5. Acts 9:1-19 _____

_____

The stories could go on and on. God forgives all who turn to Him in belief and repentance in response to His Spirit, regardless of their sin. God forgave cheating tax collectors, demoniacs, social outcasts, prostitutes, adulterers, and murderers. Patrick, too, can be forgiven.

When we confess our sin—which means we agree with God's judgment and are repenting of that sin—"He is faithful and righteous to forgive us our sins and to cleanse us from all unrighteousness" (1 John 1:9). In a supernatural, amazing way God takes the stain of our sin and makes it white as snow (Isa. 1:18)!

**Patrick needs to hear this truth again to counter the Devil's lies.
Do you? Thank God now for His forgiving love.**

"You Will Never Overcome That Sin."

Maybe you've been there. You responded to God's calling you to Him, but the temptations are stronger than ever. You fail once, twice, and then again. The doubts creep in: "I don't think I'll ever find victory over this sin. Maybe I'm just kidding myself." Doubts lead to defeat and further disobedience—and the Devil wins this round.

**Though much debate surrounds Romans 7:14-24, it appears that
Paul, too, understood the battle involved in trying to live in
Christian obedience. Read the verses below, and underline the
words that suggest this conflict.**

We know that the law is spiritual; but I am made out of flesh, sold into sin's power. For I do not understand what I am doing, because I do not practice what I want to do, but I do what I hate. And if I do what I do not want to do, I agree with the law that it is good. So now I am no longer the one doing it, but it is sin living in me. For I know that nothing good lives in me, that is, in my flesh. For the desire to do what is good is with me, but there is no ability to do it. For I do not do the good that I want to do, but I practice the evil that I do not want to do. Now if I do what I do not want, I am no longer the one doing it, but it is the sin that lives in me. So I discover this principle: when I want to do good, evil is with me. For in my inner self I joyfully agree with God's law. But I see a different law in the parts of my body, waging war against the law of my mind and taking me prisoner to the law of sin in the parts of my body. What a wretched man I am! Who will rescue me from this body of death?

Certainly you found many words that reflect Paul's battle. Even when he wanted to do good, he often did not. The battle between his old and new self remained present, and sin reared its head even when Paul longed to do right. Was there any hope for this "wretched man" in a body of death? Is there any hope for us when we are caught in our sin? Paul answered his own questions in the next verses:
- "I thank God through Jesus Christ our Lord!" (Rom. 7:25).
- "No condemnation now exists for those in Christ Jesus, because the
  Spirit's law of life in Christ Jesus has set you free from the law of sin
  and of death" (Rom. 8:1-2).

The sword of the Spirit teaches us that through Jesus and in the power of the Spirit, we have been freed from the judgment of the law, which is sin and death. Instead, we are in Christ Jesus, who promises forgiveness and restoration. We counter the Enemy's lies by trusting this truth.

"The Church Will Never Accept You Again."

When we accept God's standard and admit that we broke His law, we can confidently ask God for forgiveness. Although He forgives us for that wrong, the church is sometimes less forgiving. The Apostle Paul addressed the potential for this kind of situation in 2 Corinthians 2:5-11. Read these verses in your Bible.

Writing to the church in Corinth, Paul spoke about a church member who had been disciplined by the church for his wrongdoing. Now, the member had repented of his wrong. Paul challenged the church to forgive and restore the man, lest he "be overwhelmed by excessive grief" (v. 7). The shame of sin would only be compounded if the Corinthians added the pain of rejection after the man had repented.

More specifically, Paul warned the Corinthians that they must forgive "so that [they] may not be taken advantage of by Satan" (v. 11). To refuse to offer love, forgiveness, and grace to a repentant church member is decidedly unchristian (Eph. 4:32) and is playing the Enemy's game. If the church would not forgive such a member, it might lose him permanently from the church. The Enemy would then win a major victory, not only in the man's life but in the church's life as well.

Make restoration the goal of any disciplinary act.

Believers must counter the lie "the church will never accept you again" by making restoration the goal of any disciplinary act (see Matt. 18:15-20; Gal. 6:1). We wield the sword of the Spirit well—and neutralize the Enemy's power at least temporarily—when we closely follow the Bible's teachings about restoration.

Dan's church did just that. When Dan and his girlfriend moved in together, his pastor confronted him privately. Later, the pastor and a deacon called on him to turn from his sinful choice. When Dan still chose not to move out, the church leaders warned him that they would take his situation to the entire church.

Leaders prayed, and Dan soon ended the relationship. He publicly sought the church's forgiveness, and they graciously accepted Dan again. The Enemy loses when fallen sinners like Dan are welcomed home again.

Mark each statement as T (true) or F (false).

_____ 1. I thank God for a church that forgave me for my wrongdoing.

_____ 2. I have been guilty of judging other church members, which led to their leaving rather than being restored.

_____ 3. My offer of forgiveness to church members depends on what sin they committed.

_____ 3. I have followed others instead of studying the Word of God for myself.

_____ 4. Sometimes I've accepted the Enemy's lies and have lived in spiritual defeat.

_____ 5. I didn't realize how important the sword—God's Word— is in overcoming the Enemy's lies.

DAILY IN THE WORD
Ephesians 5:25-33

Paul turned his attention more specifically to husbands who are to love their wives "just as also Christ loved the church and gave Himself for her" (v. 25). Husbands are to be willing to die for their wives. This mandate to love wives with a sacrificial love was unusual in the ancient world, where women were devalued. Paul went against culture, even the church culture of that era, in exhorting a giving, caring, respecting love that builds up wives and leads them to spiritual growth.

Paul also used the marriage relationship as an analogy to talk about the relationship between Christ and the church. Christ gave Himself for the church, loves the church, makes the church holy, and cleanses the church to present her as holy and blameless. As the church, we are members of His body, united under His love and calling. God has now revealed this truth to us—a marvelous truth that is difficult for us to comprehend when we realize just how sinful we are.

APPLICATION
- If you are a husband, make certain you love your wife sacrificially. If you are a wife, pray for your husband every day.
- Meditate on Christ's incredible love for you. Thank Him for it.

MEMORY VERSE FOR THIS WEEK
"You were once darkness, but now you are light in the Lord. Walk as children of light." Ephesians 5:8

day *five*

PROCLAIMING THE WORD

Think about all you've been encouraged to do with the Word of God in this study. This list isn't exhaustive, but you've been challenged to read it, study it, memorize it, speak it, live it, believe it, trust it, follow it, learn it, obey it, and journal it. In this lesson, we will focus more on proclaiming the Word.

Paul typically used two Greek words that can be translated as "word" (either *logos* or *rhema*). The word he used in Ephesians 6:17 *(rhema)* often refers to the *word proclaimed,* or the spoken word.

Paul wrote that we defeat the Enemy not only by reading and knowing the Word, but also by speaking its truth. When we share the gospel, the Spirit of God uses the Word to penetrate hearts, and the Devil loses another round. The sword of the Spirit thus complements the armor that covers the feet, which also emphasizes telling the gospel of peace.

Today we will review biblical truths about warfare so that we might assuringly speak to others. Take a minute now and ask God to make you sensitive to others around you who need to hear these truths.

Christ Has Defeated the Powers

Read the different versions of Colossians 2:15 in the margin. Scholars debate the meaning of this verse, but many believe it teaches that Jesus defeated the Enemy's powers through His death on the cross.

Curtis Vaughan commented on these verses, "Christ, in this picture, is the conquering general; the powers and authorities are the vanquished enemy displayed as the spoils of battle before the entire universe. To the casual observer the cross appears to be only an instrument of death, the symbol of Christ's defeat; Paul represents it as Christ's chariot of victory."[2] Of course, Jesus' authority over the Enemy was

"When he had disarmed the rulers and authorities, He made a public display of them, having triumphed over them through Him." *NASB*

"He disarmed the rulers and authorities and disgraced them publicly; He triumphed over them by Him." *HCSB*

"And having spoiled principalities and powers, he made a shew of them openly, triumphing over them in it." *KJV*

apparent long before His death. Demons knew they were defeated before Jesus ever spoke to them (Mark 1:23-25; 5:6-8). In fact, in some cases He cast them out from a distance without speaking a word to the demons (Mark 7:24-30). Satan himself had to get permission from Jesus before sifting Peter (Luke 22:31).

We learned in previous weeks that Jesus died as the perfect, righteous sacrifice (Heb. 7:26-27) who became sin for us (2 Cor. 5:21). Having satisfied God's wrath against us (1 John 2:1-2), He publicly broke the Enemy's power through His death and resurrection. Jesus ultimately defeated Satan not by public displays of power but by His surrender to a cross (Phil. 2:5-8).

We must announce this good news to others. Maybe you know someone who is in a spiritual battle and needs to hear that Jesus has already defeated the powers. If so, write that person's name below, and pray for him or her now. Make specific plans to tell that person this good news.

The Enemy Can't Nullify God's Grace

In Zechariah 3:1-7, Zechariah reported a vision that God gave him. This vision showed God's grace for Israel, which was represented by a priest named Joshua. Read this passage in your Bible, and answer these questions.

1. Who was the accuser in this story?

2. What image indicates that Joshua was guilty and sinful?

3. Even though Joshua was guilty, did the Lord allow Satan to accuse him? ❏ yes ❏ no

4. What image shows that God forgave Joshua?

5. Was Satan strong enough to stop God from extending grace to guilty Joshua? ❏ yes ❏ no

Joshua was clearly guilty, as evidenced by his filthy garments. Satan sought to accuse him, knowing that he had sufficient grounds to do so. God, however, stepped in and rebuked the Accuser. Instead, He gave Joshua clean garments that represented His forgiveness and justification. Joshua was guilty, yet the Accuser could not stop God from extending His grace. We're all guilty of sin (Rom. 3:23), and none of us is good (Mark 10:18). Nevertheless, God graciously saves us and gives us the clean garments of His righteousness (2 Cor. 5:21). His grace is always more powerful than the Enemy's accusations. That's great news for all of us!

Years ago, I taught a Sunday School class of seventh and eighth grade guys, many of who were fairly new believers at the time. I've watched them grow and mature since then. They didn't always live godly lives. Sometimes they messed up, and often they dealt with guilt over their wrong choices. Still, many of these teenagers are now walking with God, serving faithfully in their churches, and raising godly families. Their testimonies have been stories of second chances. I'm continually thankful that the Enemy's brief victories couldn't nullify God's grace in their lives.

Think about your own story. In what ways did God make His grace known to you? How many times has He granted you a second chance? It's no wonder that we sing of God's grace as amazing.

How can we not announce that kind of good news to everyone? When we do that, we take up the sword of the Spirit and offensively move against the Enemy.

God Fights the Battle for Us

Two of the best known stories in the Old Testament are the Hebrews' crossing of the Red Sea (Ex. 14:5-31) and David's battle with Goliath (1 Sam. 17). Many Christians can tell these stories, but they often omit two powerful verses that we can't ignore. Do you know what these Scriptures report about spiritual warfare?

Read in your Bible Exodus 14:13-14 and 1 Samuel 17:46-47. What do each of these passages teach you about battles?

Exodus 14:13-14 _____

_____

1 Samuel 17:46-47 _____

_____

The battle is real, but God will accomplish His plan through the battle. Your answers should read something like Moses' words. "The LORD will fight for you" (Ex. 14:14) and David's words, "The battle is the LORD's" (1 Sam. 17:47). When we realize God fights the battles for us, we have no reason to fear or be discouraged. The ultimate outcome is never in question because no one can defeat God.

Does this truth mean that we play no role in spiritual battles? If that were the case, Paul would never have told the Ephesians (and us) to put on the full armor of God. The ultimate outcome of spiritual warfare is never in doubt, because God is all-powerful; however, our choices in the battle do affect our lives. If I choose not to live righteously (wearing the breastplate), I shouldn't be surprised if I have to pay a penalty for my unrighteous choices. It's when I try to fight my own battles that I find myself in the most trouble—though God will still somehow use that trouble to correct me, defeat the Enemy, and honor Himself.

We need to announce the good news that we have no reason to fight battles in our own power. The Word of God shows us that the almighty God who cannot be defeated fights for us. That's powerfully good news!

A Review: Wearing the Full Armor of God

Though we have one more week in our study, this lesson concludes our look at the pieces of God's armor described in Ephesians 6. Note one more time how the armor pieces can't be separated:

The almighty God who cannot be defeated fights for us.

- Wearing the belt of truth is not possible without knowing the Word— the sword of the Spirit.
- The righteousness associated with the breastplate is described in the Word.
- Our feet are sandaled with the gospel of peace found in the Word.
- The foundation for the shield of faith is the Word that proclaims God's promises on which faith is built.
- The Word of God describes the salvation associated with the helmet.

It should now be clear why Paul said we must wear the *full* armor of God. God has divinely interlinked the armor so that the pieces naturally fit together and cannot be separated. Are you wearing the whole armor of God?

> *God has divinely interlinked the armor so that the pieces naturally fit together and cannot be separated.*

DAILY IN THE WORD
Ephesians 6:1-4

After addressing the relationship between the husband and wife, Paul spoke to the parent-child relationship. Paul didn't exempt children from their responsibility to obey their parents. He reinforced this imperative by quoting the fifth commandment and its accompanying promise: "honor your father and mother … that it may go well with you" (vv. 2-3).

Paul concluded with a charge to fathers, who again were entrusted with a leadership responsibility within the family. Fathers must "bring them [children] up in the training and instruction of the Lord" (v. 4), being careful to avoid stirring their children to anger. The broad responsibilities of "bringing them up" likely included nurturing, training, warning, and teaching children. Thus, the male leader in the home has much responsibility to point his family to Christ.

APPLICATION
- Thank God for Christian parents, if that is your situation.
- Spend time this week with your children or make contact with your adult children. Tell them that you love them with the Lord's love.

MEMORY VERSE FOR THIS WEEK
"You were once darkness, but now you are light in the Lord. Walk as children of light." Ephesians 5:8

---

1. William Hendriksen, *Exposition of Galatians, Ephesians, Philippians, Colossians, and Philemon* in *New Testament Commentary* (Grand Rapids: Baker Books, 1995), 279.
2. Curtis Vaughan, "Colossians" in *The Expositor's Bible Commentary*, vol. 11 (Grand Rapids: Zondervan, 1978), 202.

❦ CASE STUDY ❦

First Church is in the process of long-range planning. Their pastor, though, wants the process to end with something more than a document that sits on a shelf. In fact, his primary concern is for the church to be ready to respond if God grants the congregation significant growth. He has appointed a lay leader, Brother Samuel, to oversee developing a plan to prepare for growth. The first meeting of Samuel's task force has just begun.

"Here's my primary concern," says Brother Samuel. "What if God blesses our church with a bunch of new believers? What if we have baby Christians running around here? Do we have a plan in place to help them grow in their faith? If not, why should God bless us with more believers?"

Brother Samuel's question hits on the foundational teachings of this study. *Putting on the Armor* is about helping believers learn to be fully-devoted disciples who are armed for battle with Satan. Based on what you have learned thus far in this study, does your church have a plan to help new believers put on the full armor of God? If not, what do you think would be essential components of this plan?

Perhaps you can think of the question this way. When you were first a believer, how do you wish your church had helped you?

Write your ideas here, and work with your study group to suggest ways that your church might better make disciples who are equipped and deployed for spiritual warfare.

The Power of Prayer

REVIEWING THE FULL ARMOR OF GOD

Belt of _____
- Know Jesus.
- Know His Word.
- Live the Word.

Breastplate of _____
- Live like Jesus.
- Make right choices.
- Resist temptation.

Feet Sandaled with the Gospel of _____
- Stand ready in faith.
- Be at peace with God.
- Be at peace with others.
- Share your faith.

Shield of _____
- Know and live the Word of God.
- Act on your faith.
- Resist worry, fear, and doubt.
- Trust the promises of God.

(continued on p. 127)

Ed Miller heard his pastor loud and clear in his Father's Day sermon: "As fathers, you should be praying with your spouse and children every day. You have the responsibility to be a spiritual leader in your home." Ed didn't question whether he should be praying with his family. But how would he achieve that goal? He and Ann were just too busy to have a predictable routine. Their daughter Reba's schedule was even more chaotic. Both of the boys were now out of the house. His own travel schedule kept him on the road. How could he *ever* pray with his family—much less every day?

In this final week of study, we'll look at the importance of prayer in spiritual warfare. The Enemy doesn't want us praying because he knows that the power of prayer is greater than his power. He often distracts us from praying simply by giving us seemingly sensible reasons not to pray.

Knowing that truth, what advice would you give to Ed Miller?

_____

_____

day *one*

PRAYING WITH URGENCY

I've listed the six pieces of the armor of God in the margins. Each piece requires that we remain faithful and obedient to Christ every day. As a review, complete this list again and draw a circle around the piece that you have had the most difficulty wearing consistently.

You've probably realized through this study that wearing the armor is never easy. Wearing it demands discipline and effort. Indeed, putting on the armor of God requires much prayer—as Paul indicated as he finished the armor of God passage (Eph. 6:18-20). Prayer isn't a piece of the armor, but it's a non-negotiable in winning spiritual battles. Prayer taps into the power of God that enables us to wear

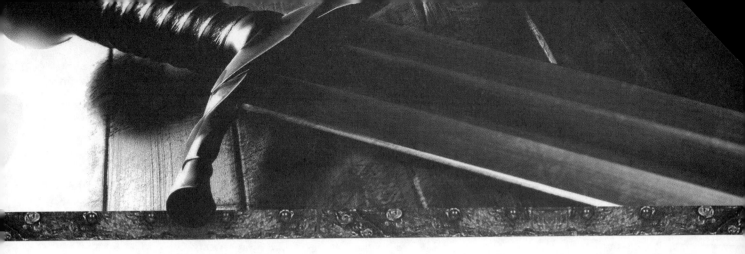

His armor. Days 1–4 of this week focus on Paul's call for prayer in Ephesians 6, and he will teach and challenge you to pray. Day 5 summarizes the entire study. Today I want to emphasize the *urgency* of prayer in spiritual warfare. Ask God to give you a passion for prayer as you read and complete the learning activities.

Pray at All Times

Read Ephesians 6:18 below. Underline any words that suggest a sense of urgency.

With every prayer and request, pray at all times in the Spirit, and stay alert in this, with all perseverance and intercession for all the saints.

Why did Paul so strongly call his readers to prayer? **First, he understood that all believers battle against the Enemy.** No follower of Jesus Christ is immune from attacks. If the Enemy was brazen enough to strike at Peter (Luke 22:31-32), Paul (2 Cor. 12:7), and Jesus Himself (Matt. 4:1-11), we shouldn't expect anything less. Those who fail to recognize the reality of the battle are the most deceived of believers.

Second, Paul knew the potential intensity of the attack. In 2 Corinthians 12, he used the word translated *buffeting* or *tormenting* to describe an attack from the Devil (v. 7). The word he used here literally means "to be slapped back and forth." The attack Paul faced was repeated, relentless, and ruthless. Paul knew the importance of believers praying for others who might face the same kind of assault.

Third, Paul expected believers to rejoice always (1 Thess. 5:16), even when under attack from the Enemy (2 Cor. 12:8-10). He had learned from his own battles with his thorn in the flesh how to rejoice despite them. He pleaded with God to remove the thorn when he was being tormented, but God told him no. In the end, Paul learned that God's grace was sufficient for him, and he even rejoiced in "catastrophes, in persecutions, and in pressures" (v. 10). Paul wanted other believers to rejoice, but such a response to difficulties seldom happens apart from others praying for us.

Fourth, Paul understood the brevity of life. He wrote the letter to the Ephesians from a jail cell, not knowing if he would live or die. He never wanted to miss an opportunity to glorify Christ, so he sought the prayers of others (Eph. 6:19-20).

As I write this study, I have been reminded that life is uncertain. My wife's uncle succumbed rapidly to cancer. A young person I know unexpectedly died. A friend with a premature infant faces a long period of hospitalization. We really don't know from day to day what life will bring us. These kinds of events always lead us to

Helmet of _____
- Understand who you were prior to salvation, and appreciate God's grace.
- Meditate upon, and marvel at God's love and holiness shown in the cross.
- Live in the assurance of Christ's return.

Sword of the _____
- Read, know, and live the Word of God.
- Speak the good news to others.

Those who fail to recognize the reality of the battle are the most deceived of believers.

pray with urgency. But Paul called for prayer "at all times … with all perserverance" because he knew Christian life is *always* a battle.

On a scale of 1-10, rank the urgency of your typical prayers.

1	2	3	4	5	6	7	8	9	10
not at all			somewhat urgent			urgent			very urgent

Be on the Alert

Compare the two Scriptures below, and notice their obvious similarities. Record your observations in the margin.

With every prayer and request, pray at all times in the Spirit, and stay alert in this, with all perseverance and intercession for all the saints (Eph. 6:18).

Devote yourselves to prayer; stay alert in it with thanksgiving (Col. 4:2).

The Apostle Paul wrote both of these texts that call for believers to *be alert* in prayer. The word Paul used here means "to watch or to give strict attention" to something. In the garden of Gethsemane (Matt. 26:38,40-41), Jesus used a synonym of this word. There, Jesus warned His disciples to stay alert lest they enter into temptation. Jesus and the disciples would be facing incredible battles in the hours to come, and He needed them to be praying with urgency.

Peter, too, spoke of being alert: "Be sober! Be on the alert! Your adversary the Devil is prowling around like a roaring lion, looking for anyone he can devour" (1 Pet. 5:8). Peter knew by experience the danger of letting down his spiritual guard. We also should stand alert, both to our situations and on behalf of others.

Recognizing the Enemy's schemes—and being ever alert to those wiles—helps us guard against the Enemy's attacks. In fact, some scholars suggest that "being alert" in Ephesians 6 and Colossians 4 refers to knowing what is going on around us so that we will pray more fervently for others. One writer warned, "Those who are not 'alert' but listless and indifferent to what is going on in their homes, cities, states, provinces, countries, churches, denominations, or in the world at large will have a very restricted prayer life."[1]

I have a picture titled "Spiritual Warfare" hanging in my office. The picture portrays a father praying at the bedside of his sleeping child while angels hover nearby. That prayer may take place at bedtime, but the wise father knows his child will face many spiritual attacks during the daylight hours. The father armed for battle always stands alert and prays with urgency on behalf of his child.

Check any of these persons who have stood alert in prayer on your behalf. Thank God for each one.

____ grandparents	____ parents	____ pastor
____ Bible study teacher	____ friend	____ schoolteacher
____ professor	____ spouse	____ coworker

Pray Urgently for Others Before the Attack

Think about your church's prayer list. In most cases, the people on a church prayer list are already sick, hurting, or under spiritual attack. We pray for families only after they are facing troubles. Our prayers for young people increase when we hear that they have made bad decisions. We pray for churches when word comes that their members are quarreling. The Devil works, and *then* we start praying.

Certainly, we should pray for people under attack, but often our prayers are only catching up with what the Enemy is doing. We pray reactively rather than proactively. Perhaps if we continually and urgently interceded for others as Paul requested the Ephesians do, the Enemy would win fewer battles.

For whom should you be praying now, before the Enemy attacks? And who is praying for you? In the words of my students, "Who's got your back covered?" Whose backs are you personally guarding?

We challenge you to end this lesson by making these commitments:
- Seek God's guidance to enlist two prayer partners from outside your family who will pray for you *every* day for at least a month after this study is completed. Ask them to pray proactively for you, trusting that their prayers will make a difference when you face spiritual attack. These partners may be some who have been praying for you since you began this study.
- Ask God to show you two other persons for whom you should pray every day. Make a commitment to be alert on their behalf and to intercede for them with perseverance.
- When God gives you direction, list the names of these persons below, and review your commitment to them monthly.

Those praying for me: | Those for whom I'm praying:

_____ | _____

_____ | _____

> Perhaps if we continually and urgently interceded for others, the Enemy would win fewer battles.

🌿 DAILY IN THE WORD 🌿
Ephesians 6:5-9

In this last section of the household codes, Paul turned his attention to relationships between slaves and masters. These verses should not be considered an affirmation of slavery. While not rejecting slavery outright, Paul called for a mutual submission of slave and master that would have been extraordinary in his world. Christian slaves were to "render service with a good attitude, as to the Lord and not to men" (v. 7). Likewise, masters were to treat slaves with respect and dignity because they knew that the Master to whom we are accountable has no favorites. He loves the slave and master alike.

The parallel for us may be our boss/employee relationships. Respect for employers and employees should characterize all believers. We are to work as "slaves of Christ," even when no one but God sees.

APPLICATION
- Perform an act of kindness this week for your boss or employees.
- Try to adopt this way of thinking: "I am doing my job for God and not for others."

MEMORY VERSE FOR THIS WEEK
"Put on the full armor of God so that you can stand against the tactics of the Devil." Ephesians 6:11

day *two*

PRAYING AT ALL TIMES IN THE SPIRIT

I travel often throughout the year. Preaching sermons, leading conferences, and attending academic meetings require me to be away from Louisville quite often. In addition, I work with churches through my consulting company. Sometimes my travel seems long and the hotel rooms get lonely.

It's always easier when my wife Pam travels with me. When she can't go, however, I know she supports me with her prayers. I love hearing her say, "I'm praying for you" as I head out to do ministry, because I know she means what she says. In fact, I know she prays for me all the time.

As I've mentioned before in this study, my wife walks with God. Her heart reflects the Holy Spirit of God. I am certain the Father hears her prayers as she prays for me day in and day out. I'm even more convinced that I couldn't do what I do apart from the strength gained through Pam's prayers.

The goal of this lesson is to learn to pray as Paul called the Ephesians to pray—at all times and in the Holy Spirit.

Pray at All Times

Review Paul's words from Ephesians 6:18 in the margin. Paul's call to "pray at all times" was a common one for him, though he used different terms to express the same idea. "Be persistent in prayer," he wrote to the Romans (Rom. 12:12). As we learned in day 1, he called the Colossians to "devote" themselves to prayer (Col. 4:2). "Pray constantly," was his word to the Thessalonians (1 Thess. 5:17). Moreover, Paul did what he asked other believers to do.

Describe what the following verses say about Paul's prayer life.

Ephesians 1:16 _____

Colossians 1:9 _____

"With every prayer and request, pray at all times in the Spirit, and stay alert in this, with all perseverance and intercession for all the saints."
Ephesians 6:18

1 Thessalonians 1:2; 3:10 _____

2 Timothy 1:3 _____

What does it mean to pray the way that Paul did? Paul said that he prayed constantly, without stopping, at all times, day and night, for other believers. Certainly, he didn't literally pray without stopping (or he could not have written the very letters that we're studying!).

Praying at all times means living in such a way that nothing hinders our prayers. What keeps us from praying? If it's self-dependence, Paul knew what it was to be broken (2 Cor. 12:7-10). If it's unconfessed sin, Paul understood the need for holy living (Eph. 4–6). If a lack of faith keeps us from praying, Paul considered everything loss if he did not know Christ by faith (Phil. 3:8-9). Paul simply lived for Christ, and nothing in his life blocked his prayer channel to God.

Praying at all times means being ever aware of the needs of others. Paul prayed for the Ephesians, the Thessalonians, the Romans, and Timothy. He urged that prayers be lifted for all men (1 Tim. 2:1-2). Paul, who willingly became "all things to all people" that some might be saved (1 Cor. 9:22), remained ever alert to the needs of others; he didn't miss opportunities to pray for them.

Sometimes we get so busy doing good "stuff" that we miss the hurting people around us. How aware are you of the needs of others around you? your neighbors? your coworkers? What hinders you from praying at all times?

Praying at all times also means praying for others before they face trouble. As we learned in day 1, we miss this simple truth so often! Praying at all times hinders the Enemy's work. An outwardly focused life that recognizes the needs of others avoids the self-centeredness that characterizes the Devil. Praying at all times results in victory for us and for others. The righteous living that makes prayer effective is the essence of wearing the breastplate of righteousness.

Mark each of the following statements true *(T)* or false *(F)*.

1. _____ As far as I can tell, nothing is hindering my prayers right now.
2. _____ My self-sufficiency probably keeps me from praying at all times.
3. _____ Sometimes it's easy for me to get so self-centered that my prayers are all about me.
4. _____ I need to practice praying at all times.
5. _____ I need the shield of faith to believe God answers my prayers.

Pray in the Spirit

For Paul, the Spirit of God was central to effective Christian living. Through Christ and by the Holy Spirit we have access to the Father (Eph. 2:18). The Spirit is working in us to make us the dwelling place of God (Eph. 2:22). In fact, the Spirit fills us (Eph. 5:18) and verifies that we are the children of God (Rom. 8:14-17). Praying in the Spirit means living in the very presence of the God to whom we speak.

The Spirit of God points out sin and righteousness while also warning us of judgment to come (John 16:7-11). He seals us as the children of God, and we are to be careful not to grieve Him (Eph. 1:13; 4:30). He is the Spirit of truth who guides us into all truth (John 16:13). Because the Holy Spirit indwells us, seals us, guides us, warns us, and teaches us, we have the power to live in victory over the Enemy. For that reason, praying in the Spirit means following God in such a way that the Father is pleased to respond to our prayers.

Praying in the Spirit means living in the very presence of the God to whom we speak.

The Holy Spirit's praying helps us when we face battles and challenges that make prayer difficult. Read Romans 8:26-39 and fill in the blanks.

• When we don't know how to pray, the _____ takes up the praying for us.

• The Spirit always conforms our prayers to the will of _____.

• The Father's will is that we be conformed to the image of His

_____.

• God will work out the details so that all things work together

for the _____ of those who love Him.

• Not even principalities nor _____ can keep us from the love of God.

Do you understand the process of praying? When we don't even know how to pray, the Holy Spirit takes our prayers and makes them effective. He, being God Himself, conforms our prayers to the will of the Father. The Father's will is that we become more like Jesus, and He uses even the difficult times in our lives to accomplish His will. The Spirit thus leads us through the battle into the position where God would have us to be. Sometimes praying in the Spirit means being so broken and dependent that only the Holy Spirit knows how to pray in our situation.

Think about this truth again. Jesus, our intercessor (Heb. 7:25), prays us through the battle when He gives the Enemy permission to sift us (Luke 22:32). Now we add another piece to this puzzle: when we don't know how to pray, the Holy Spirit takes up the praying in our place. With Jesus and the Holy Spirit involved in the praying, how can we not trust that God will use our battles to accomplish His plan? Even principalities and powers can't separate us from God!

Think of a difficult time when you seemingly could not even pray, but God heard the cries of your heart anyway. Consider the miracle that took place when God the Father, Son, and Holy Spirit responded to you. How would you describe that time?

_____

_____

_____

_____

_____

When we don't know how to pray, the Holy Spirit takes up the praying in our place.

DAILY IN THE WORD
Ephesians 6:10-13

As Paul continued the practical portion of his book, he instructed his readers how to fight the battles of spiritual warfare. He began by commanding them to "be strengthened by the Lord and by His vast strength" (v. 10). Paul reminded the Ephesians that the Lord gave them His strength for their own, empowering them in spiritual battles against numerous powers (rulers, authorities, world powers, and spiritual forces).

The proper response is to "put on the full armor of God so that you can stand against the tactics of the Devil" (v. 11). The Devil is a scheming opponent, but God gives His armor to believers. In His armor, we can resist Satan's powers, stand against the Enemy, and win the battles against temptation that we fight every day.

The English language doesn't show it, but the commands in these verses are plural. Individuals do put on the armor, but we are in this war together.

APPLICATION
- Thank God for the strength that He alone gives us.
- If you face a battle this week, remember that the battle is His.

MEMORY VERSE FOR THIS WEEK
"Put on the full armor of God so that you can stand against the tactics of the Devil." Ephesians 6:11

day **three**

PRAYING FOR ALL THE SAINTS

Yesterday I talked about my wife Pam who prays for me continually. Pam is my greatest prayer warrior, but I could have spoken about many others. My younger brother, Allen, touches heaven when he prays. Shirley, a long-time friend, has shared many a prayer burden with my wife and me. Sonney, who has now gone to be with the Lord, prayed for me when I was his young, naïve pastor at age 20. Now, my students pray with me and for me as we encourage one another in ministry.

This lesson completes our look at Paul's command to pray "at all times in the Spirit … for all the saints" (Eph. 6:18). Today we'll learn the importance of praying intentionally and persistently.

We face intensely real
battles; and timid, ineffective
pray-ers must learn to pray
with faith and power.

Put on the Armor and Pray

Think about the order of this study. Paul called the Ephesians to put on the full armor of God, knowing they were in a spiritual war (Eph. 6:11-12). Their enemies, he said, were not flesh and blood. Next, he described for them the armor of God (6:14-17). Then, he challenged them to pray for each other and for him (6:18-20).

The order of the commands makes sense. To the same believers he challenged to pray for him, Paul said, "Put on the full armor of God." He knew that prayers are most effective when prayed by righteous believers (John 15:7; Jas. 5:16). Truth, righteousness, and faith characterize putting on the armor. Paul understood that those who are wearing the full armor of God make the best prayer warriors.

This approach makes even more sense when we recall where Paul was as he wrote Ephesians. As a prisoner for his faith, Paul wasn't interested in the number of people praying for him, but he was in the faith of those people. He needed prayer partners who moved heaven and threatened hell. Keep in mind that we need both the prayers of faithful believers and to be fully armed prayer warriors.

I trust that as you have learned how to put on the armor of God, you're more prepared to pray for others than you were at the beginning of this study. We face intensely real battles; and timid, ineffective pray-ers must learn to pray with faith and power. Remember that God wants to answer our prayers on behalf of others as well as ourselves. Those who are equipped in the armor of God are also the ones most likely to be deployed. God knows He can trust them in the battle.

On the scales evaluate how you've grown in your prayer life during this study. On a scale of 1 to 10, circle the number to indicate how well prepared you were/are to be an effective prayer warrior.

At the beginning of this study:

1	2	3	4	5	6	7	8	9	10
not well at all									very well

Now:

1	2	3	4	5	6	7	8	9	10
not well at all									very well

Get a Plan to Pray for All the Saints

Remember that we put on the armor of God so that we can "stand against the tactics of the Devil" (Eph. 6:11). To counter this Schemer, we need a plan to pray for "all the saints" before the Devil gets a foothold in our lives and our churches (Eph. 4:27). Here are some simple strategies to pray for other believers:
- Pray through your church's directory. Focus on a few families each week, and pray intentionally for each one over the course of a year.
- Pray for each of the churches in your local area, interceding for them as you drive past their buildings each week.
- Pray for all of the Christian schoolteachers in your local school district.
- Pray systematically for all of the local church pastors in your city. The Yellow Pages directory might serve as a guide.

- Using your church's calendar, pray for the believers involved in each event on the schedule.
- Go to the Web sites for the North American Mission Board (www.namb.net) and the International Mission Board (www.imb.org), and pray for missionaries whose stories are told there.
- Use the time prior to your church's worship service (when everyone else is talking) to pray for members you see.
- Prayerwalk through your church building and pray for the believers who will sit in each chair or pew.
- Every Monday, pray for your church's staff and their families.
- Pray for every member of your Sunday School class or small group.

You get the point: we best counter the Enemy by beating him to the punch. Our strategy to cover believers in prayer might not remove them from the battle, but it may well help them to be faithful in the battle.

Take a look at the suggested prayer ideas again, and check one or two you might build into your personal prayer strategy. Perhaps you know of other intentional ways to pray for others. If so, write them here and be prepared to share them with your group.

_____

_____

Get a Plan and Persevere

Read Ephesians 6:18 in the margin. We haven't yet considered a critical issue in the spiritual battles associated with praying for others: the issue of *perseverance*. Frankly, praying for others is hard work, and you might want to give up. It's easy to fall asleep on the watch just as Jesus' own disciples did (Luke 22:45-46). Consider the obstacles that you face in this task of keeping your commitment current.

Circle any obstacles you face when thinking about praying for others. Then, put an "x" by the one that is most difficult for you.

lack of concern—I don't care like I should.

lack of discipline—I don't make the time.

lack of knowledge—I don't know their needs.

lack of faith—I don't believe my prayers will make a difference.

lack of timing in prayer—I don't pray on the front end of an attack.

lack of in-depth relationships—I don't know most people that well.

lack of a plan—I have no strategy to pray each day.

other _____

PRAYER RESOURCES

Serving in Your Church Prayer Ministry by Chuck Lawless

A House of Prayer: Prayer Ministries in Your Church by John Franklin

And the Place Was Shaken by John Franklin

Disciple's Prayer Life: Walking in Fellowship with God by T.W. Hunt

"With every prayer and request, pray at all times in the Spirit, and stay alert in this, with all perseverance and intercession for all the saints." *Ephesians 6:18*

When we recognize the obstacles, we understand why we find it difficult to persevere when praying for others. We persevere only when our hearts are committed to other people. We certainly won't "pray on" if we lack concern or are self-centered. Nor will we persevere in prayer if we have holes in our armor. The Enemy will quickly find our vulnerable places. His attacks on us mount, and it's easy to become discouraged. The Enemy always wins a skirmish when we stop praying.

Maybe you've been praying for another believer for some time. For example, I've served as pastor to church members who were praying diligently for a wayward child to return to God. Even parents sometimes think about giving up when discouragement sets in.

You might be praying for other believers who themselves have become discouraged under attack. Some get angry with God for allowing the attack. Others fall back into patterns of sin, almost in deliberate rebellion against the God who didn't "help" them. Still others withdraw from the church. You know that all of these are making poor decisions, yet they fall increasingly into despair. Our frustration with them in our humanity makes praying for them difficult.

Or perhaps you're just now thinking about praying more strategically for other believers *before* they face attack. If so, realize that Satan wants you to forget about your commitment. He wants you to let down your prayer shield around others and not pray for them again until after he strikes.

In any of these cases, *don't* let the Enemy win! Put on the armor, get a plan, and persevere in prayer for all the saints.

> *Don't* let the Enemy win! Put on the armor, get a plan, and persevere in prayer for all the saints.

> Knowing truth is one step to victory, but using truth to make right choices is vital.

DAILY IN THE WORD
Ephesians 6:14-17

Yesterday we reviewed the importance of wearing the "full armor of God" as we take our stand against the Enemy. In today's text Paul continued by listing each piece of the armor worn in the battle.

First, we should wear truth like a belt around our waist. Second, we wear righteousness like armor on our chest. Knowing truth is one step to victory, but using truth to make right choices is vital. Third, we wear the gospel of peace, which brings peace in our relationship with others and God.

Fourth, we "take up the shield of faith" which will help us trust God during the difficult moments of the war (v. 16). Fifth, we "take the helmet of salvation" (v. 17). Apart from experiencing salvation in Christ, we will find victory impossible. Finally, we take up the "sword of the Spirit which is God's Word" (v. 17).

APPLICATION
- Review again the armor you are wearing. Is there a part missing?
- Thank God for His armor you wear on a daily basis, and ask Him to supply any missing parts.

MEMORY VERSE FOR THIS WEEK
"Put on the full armor of God so that you can stand against the tactics of the Devil." Ephesians 6:11

day **four**

THE ENEMY AND PRAYER

Think of a person in your church known as a prayer warrior. Have you ever wished to be called a prayer warrior too? Perhaps you think it will happen when the kids leave home, after you retire, or when desperation forces you to your knees.

Prayer is one of the most difficult spiritual disciplines to develop. Bible study plans allow us to check off the chapters we read, but no such "plan" exists with prayer. We can set parameters for fasting such as one day a week. Evaluating the discipline of giving is fairly simple (just count the dollars!), but you can't "count up" your prayers. Your prayer life is more subjective because prayer is ongoing.

Who's to say how much or how often you should pray? Prayer demands discipline—and that's hard work even *before* the Enemy gets involved. It's easy to miss a morning quiet time and assume we have missed our chance for that day.

As we've been studying the importance of prayer in spiritual warfare, day 4 will help us think about hindrances to our prayers. While the Enemy may not be directly attacking us in these ways, we should always stay alert to these hindrances and know how to defeat them before they defeat us.

Self-Sufficiency Hinders Our Praying

Do you recall the story of the father whose faith struggled when the disciples couldn't cast a demon out of his son? In week 4 we looked at this father's honest faith. Another part of this story, though, considers the floundering disciples.

Read Mark 9:14-29 again and answer these questions.

How long had the boy been possessed? _____

Were the disciples successful at exorcising the demon? ❏ yes ❏ no

Was Jesus successful at exorcising the demon? ❏ yes ❏ no

What was Jesus' answer when His disciples asked why they could not cast out the demon?

_____

_____

As you've read, the disciples failed in their attempt to exorcise the demon that had been tormenting the young boy since he was a child. Jesus, of course, took care of the problem. The disciples then used their first opportunity to ask Jesus about their failure. His response was clear: "This kind can come out by nothing but prayer."[2]

Jesus implied that the disciples had somehow attempted to cast out a demon *without* praying. They had apparently tried to take on the Enemy in their own strength, and failed. As a result, a boy remained in demonic bondage, and a father struggled with believing.

Why would the disciples have tried an exorcism without praying? They had previously been successful at exorcising demons (Mark 6:7-13). We can't be certain, but maybe they thought yesterday's power was sufficient for today's battle. After all, if they had been victorious in the past, surely they would still have that power today—even without praying. Their self-sufficiency led to quick defeat when the demon apparently did not budge at their command.

Before we judge the disciples too harshly, we need to evaluate how often we live out of our own strength. I can think of many times when the Lord had to show me that I was fighting today's spiritual battles on the basis of yesterday's victories. Self-sufficiency pleases the Enemy, for without God's blessings we can do nothing of eternal significance. How often have you been guilty—as I have been—of going to God only *after* you figured out that you couldn't handle the issues on your own?

Check (✔) the statement that best describes your current approach to prayer.

❑ Praying throughout the day comes naturally for me.
❑ I am learning to pray at all times of the day, but I still pray more often when I face trouble.
❑ I do much in my own power, and I pray only when I can't handle a difficult situation.
❑ I don't pray enough in any situation.

Sin Hinders Our Praying

Read Isaiah 59:1-2 in the margin. The Hebrews were looking for God's intervention on their behalf. However, God told them that their lifestyles didn't show that they wanted Him to lead them. After all, they were living in disobedience.

The prophet's words are clear—God wasn't responding to the prayers of His people who were living in sin. He chooses whom to hear. This truth should make us think twice before we yield to temptation.

When my wife and I prepared to sell our first home, we were sure it would be snatched up by eager buyers. It was clean and the yard was well-kept. We set the price to sell quickly. In fact, you couldn't find another house in our area that was as nice as ours at that price. And sure enough, a young couple made us an offer in the first week we had it on the market.

We soon learned, however, that termites and water beneath our house had caused a great deal of damage to the flooring. Our house looked great from the floor up, but the floors themselves had been seriously damaged by unseen problems. That damage—even though it was unseen—cost us several thousand dollars.

Sin works in a similar way. We might look holy in church and among other Christians (that is, from the floor up) while hidden sin rots the foundation of our lives. In the end, unconfessed controlling sin makes our prayers fruitless. We gain the temporary pleasure of sin while we lose the eternal pleasure of knowing that God hears us when we pray. The Enemy rejoices when we settle for the little he offers, and we render our prayers ineffective in the process.

Maybe the disciples thought yesterday's power was sufficient for today's battle.

"Indeed, the LORD's hand is not too short to save, and His ear is not too deaf to hear. But your iniquities have built barriers between you and your God, and your sins have made Him hide His face from you so that He does not listen."
Isaiah 59:1-2

Read Matthew 6:13 and Luke 22:39-46, and then answer the following questions.

According to Jesus, when should we pray about temptation?

_____

_____

When do we *usually* pray about temptation?

_____

_____

How might our battles with sin change if we prayed as Jesus taught us?

_____

_____

_____

Jesus taught us to pray that God would deliver us from the Evil One. He also taught us to pray for God's protection *before* we face a temptation. Do you think we might stand against the Enemy more effectively if we were to follow Jesus' directions?

Poor Relationships Hinder Our Praying

In week 3 we looked at the importance of forgiving others so that we don't give the Enemy a foothold in our lives. Let's return to that topic as it relates to prayer. First Peter 3:7 tells husbands to show their wives honor "so that your prayers will not be hindered." Specifically, God expects husbands to unselfishly give honor to their wives. Anything less results in prayers that are just words.

Why is God so concerned about our marriages? The marriage relationship is a picture of Christ's love for His church (Eph. 5:22-33). The world should see Christ in us when they see how we love our spouses. At times, though, our selfish choices mar that picture. Marriage becomes more about us than about our spouses, and we forget that we are modeling Christ's love for the church to our friends, family, and coworkers. God isn't pleased, and our prayers are consequently hindered.

Even within marriage we sometimes hold on to bitterness and anger. Maybe you still remember the hurtful sting of something your spouse said or did, and thinking about those actions brings back hard feelings. You might even bring up the incident months or years later when another argument erupts. Those angry feelings affect not only our relationship with one another but also our relationship with God (Matt. 6:14-15).

Jesus warned us that we can't pray effectively if we haven't forgiven others who have hurt us (Mark 11:25). Forgiving one's spouse is especially important since marriage reflects Christian love! The Enemy, of course, wants us to stay bitter and unforgiving toward others. When we follow his lead, our prayers accomplish little.

Jesus taught us to pray for God's protection *before* we face a temptation.

As we finish this lesson, write one action you will take in response to these teachings about hindrances to prayer.

self-sufficiency _____

_____

_____

sin _____

_____

_____

poor relationships _____

_____

_____

More In-depth Study
Read these verses and, in the margin, list the hindrances to prayer they describe: Matthew 6:5-6; James 1:5-8; James 4:2-3.

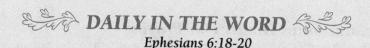

DAILY IN THE WORD
Ephesians 6:18-20

Paul understood that those believers who wear the armor of God and walk in victory need prayer support. For this reason he challenged the Ephesians to pray "with all perseverance and intercession for all the saints" (v. 18). When holy believers pray consistently for each other, they best equip the church for the battles she faces. The result is a church that stands strong.

Paul then asked these believers to pray for him, specifically that he would be bold enough to speak the gospel as he should. He was imprisoned for that very reason, yet he sought prayer that he would keep preaching boldly. He remained an ambassador for Christ even while in chains. We may never be imprisoned like Paul, but we too should long for believers to pray for us in this manner.

APPLICATION
• Pray intentionally for two believers this week.
• Ask two believers to pray for your boldness.

MEMORY VERSE FOR THIS WEEK
"Put on the full armor of God so that you can stand against the tactics of the Devil." Ephesians 6:11

day   *five*

EQUIPPED AND DEPLOYED?

You may live near a military base. If so, you know that deployment often means being sent to the front lines. Men and women who are deployed aren't just practicing drills anymore. They are facing the real deal, and their lives are at stake.

The title of this study is *Putting on the Armor: Equipped and Deployed for Spiritual Warfare.* For the last seven weeks, we have studied together the armor that God gives us for spiritual battles. We've also been talking about being equipped (by putting on the armor), but we haven't talked much about being deployed. In this final lesson we will concentrate on the entire second component of the subtitle!

Day 5 will bring together the equipping and deploying aspects of this study. In fact, you'll discover that we *have* been talking about both equipping and deploying from the beginning. First, ask yourself this question: If you feel equipped with the full armor of God and wear these elements of warfare on a consistent basis, when are you deployed into combat?

Deployment Requires Getting the Armor Ready

Suppose you were the commanding officer of a military platoon, and orders came that your troops would soon be deployed. How would you prepare? Would you want to make certain they had the proper armaments for the battle? Of course, a capable and wise officer would want to provide the troops with the best weaponry available. Anything less would be potential suicide for the soldiers.

Compare that reality to the spiritual battles we face. Our marching orders are clear: we are to glorify God by carrying out the calling of the Great Commission (Matt. 28:18-20) to reach everyone to the ends of the earth with the message of salvation. That work includes preaching the gospel to nonbelievers and the all-encompassing work of making disciples of those who come to believe. Accomplishing this task is made harder because the Enemy fights against us all the way. For that reason, we must have the right armor for the battle.

Based on this study and your reading of Ephesians, mark each statement true (*T*) or false (*F*).

1. _____ The armor we wear is God's armor.
2. _____ The God who gives us His armor is more powerful than the Enemy we face.
3. _____ The Enemy can't go further than God allows him to go.
4. _____ God ultimately uses any outcome for His glory.
5. _____ We've been given all the armor we need to win spiritual battles.

It probably didn't take you long to realize that all of the statements are true. The armor we wear isn't ours. It belongs to the true God for whom the Enemy is no match. God has given us His truth, righteousness, peace, faith, salvation, and the Word. What else do we need for this battle? To follow the analogy, our commanding officer has provided for us all the armor we need when we are deployed.

Deployment: Equipping Invites Attack

Before being deployed, a nation's soldiers train, prepare, rehearse, and then train some more in preparation for the battle. The training is non-negotiable, an imperative that has saved lives and led to many military victories. A deployed troop that is untrained poses little threat.

In general warfare, the equipping component is seldom as much a threat to the enemy as the deployment. A soldier learning to toss a grenade is less of a threat than a trained warrior who pulls the pin and tosses the weapon across enemy lines.

In spiritual warfare, both the equipping and training threaten the Enemy. In the spiritual arena deployment starts with equipping, but the battle is already underway. Perhaps an illustration will help clarify this point. Suppose my marching orders as a soldier of Christ are to evangelize the lost (as they are for all believers). My orders and my preparation and equipping would look something like this:

MY ORDERS: To tell others about Jesus

MY PREPARATION/EQUIPPING TO CARRY OUT MY ORDERS:
1. Reading the Word to know the story of Jesus means …
   • I must take up the Sword through Bible study.
   • I must learn truth (the belt).
   • I must live righteously to affirm the life-changing nature of this story (the breastplate).
2. Knowing how to tell the story means …
   • I must understand the good news of salvation (the helmet).
   • I must know how to speak truth (the belt and the sword).
   • I must know how to trust God as I go tell (the shield of faith).
   • I must be prepared to proclaim the gospel of peace (feet sandaled).

Do you see the point? Certainly, just evangelism itself threatens the Enemy. But the Enemy doesn't stand by silently. He doesn't want me to get ready to witness by learning truth, living righteously, preparing to speak the good news, trusting the promises of God, living out my own salvation, and believing the Word.

In that sense, the battle has begun before I ever follow my orders to evangelize. Equipping puts me in the war, and I am consequently deployed from the beginning. My choice to follow my deployment orders to evangelize only heats up a battle already begun. We are continuously in this spiritual war, whether we realize it or not.

Deployment Means Being Faithful

Here's a truth you may not want to know: you might face more serious spiritual battles than you've ever faced simply because you have taken this study (and I can hear you now, wondering why I didn't warn you seven weeks ago!). The Enemy never likes it when we put on the armor of God.

On the other hand, God delights when we wear His armor. As we have seen throughout this study, putting on the armor is about Christian obedience. When we walk in daily obedience, we please God and threaten the Enemy. Simple obedience is the foundational victory in spiritual warfare.

In spiritual warfare, both the equipping and training threaten the Enemy.

Moreover, we please God when we learn to trust Him to give us the victory (remember, the armor is His). That victory, of course, may not always come as we expect or want. In fact, sometimes victory might seem like defeat in the world's eyes—as in persecution, for example. Nevertheless, the God of eternity can take seeming defeat and reap His glory from it. The Devil isn't powerful enough to keep God from getting the honor He deserves.

If that's the case, we have no reason not to march ahead for God's glory. We accept God's deployment because He has equipped us in His armor. Should the Devil attack us with temptation and we fend him off with the armor, we win through God's grace. If God deploys us to the ends of the earth with the gospel of peace, we press on in His armor. When the Devil strikes at our homes and our relationships, we don't give up or give in; rather, we put on the full armor and pray our families through the conflict.

And, should the Devil get permission to persecute us until death, we rely on the sword of the Spirit that promises us His presence at all times (Heb. 13:5). In no case does the Enemy ultimately win when God has equipped and deployed us in His service.

Go, then, and press on in the battle for the glory of God!

> The Devil isn't powerful enough to keep God from getting the honor He deserves.

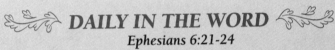

DAILY IN THE WORD
Ephesians 6:21-24

In today's final reading, Paul concluded his letter with personal remarks about his friend Tychicus. Tychicus was sent to the Ephesians not only to deliver Paul's letter, but also to encourage the church and update them about Paul. Private messengers often delivered such personal letters in the first century.

Finally, Paul ended the epistle with a closing benediction. "Peace" and "grace" remind us of the greeting at the beginning of this letter. Paul closed the letter by extending a word of peace, love, and grace to all "who have undying love for our Lord Jesus Christ" (v. 24). In this book that recognizes the reality of a spiritual battle, Paul affirmed that we can still experience victory in Christ. This truth encouraged the original readers of Paul's letter, and it should encourage us today.

APPLICATION
- Write a note of encouragement to someone.
- Thank God for the love, grace, and peace that He gives you.

MEMORY VERSE FOR THIS WEEK
"Put on the full armor of God so that you can stand against the tactics of the Devil." Ephesians 6:11

---

1. William Hendricksen, "Ephesians," *New Testament Commentary* (Grand Rapids: Baker, 1996), 281.
2. Some versions read "prayer and fasting."

Linking the Armor Group Activity

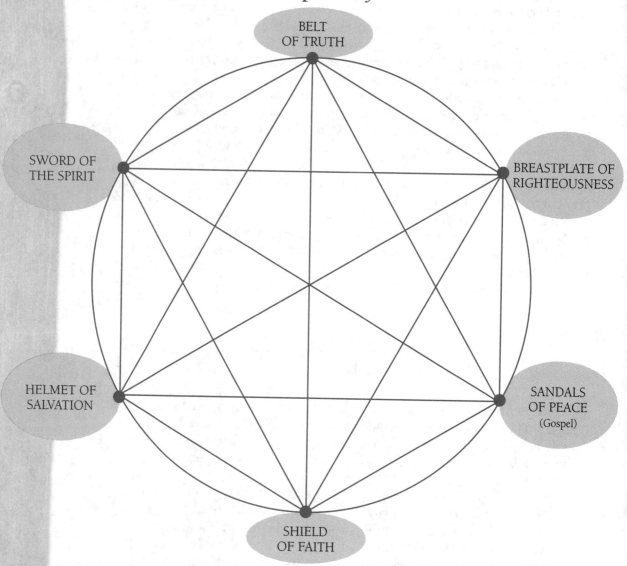

Use pages 126-27 to review the components of each piece of armor. There are 15 paired links or connections among the pieces of the armor of God. In groups of two or three, identify how your assigned pieces of armor relate to one another. Answer the questions posed by your facilitator.

1. Belt of Truth / Breastplate of Righteousness
2. Belt of Truth / Sandals of Peace
3. Belt of Truth / Shield of Faith
4. Belt of Truth / Helmet of Salvation
5. Belt of Truth / Sword of the Spirit
6. Breastplate of Righteousness / Sandals of Peace
7. Breastplate of Righteousness / Shield of Faith
8. Breastplate of Righteousness / Helmet of Salvation
9. Breastplate of Righteousness / Sword of the Spirit
10. Sandals of Peace / Shield of Faith
11. Sandals of Peace / Helmet of Salvation
12. Sandals of Peace / Sword of the Spirit
13. Shield of Faith / Helmet of Salvation
14. Shield of Faith / Sword of the Spirit
15. Helmet of Salvation / Sword of the Spirit

KNOW-BE-DO Group Activity

"Put on the full armor of God so that you can stand against the tactics of the Devil" (Eph. 6:11).

For each piece of armor, describe what believers must KNOW about the piece of armor, what they must BE in order to effectively wear the piece, and what specific actions (DO) result when a believer wears the piece of armor. Relate last week's memory verse to your assigned piece of armor. As other groups report, complete your chart.

ARMOR	KNOW	BE	DO
Belt of Truth			
Breastplate of Righteousness			
Sandals of the Gospel of Peace			
Shield of Faith			
Helmet of Salvation			
Sword of the Spirit			

The Next Steps

You may remember that the Enemy's goal is to entice us to mess up or to give up. We mess up when we fall into sin, and we generally give up when we get discouraged. Sometimes, though, we give up because we have no plan for continued growth. We don't know the next steps, so we take no steps—and no steps are the equivalent of decline in spiritual growth.

At your group's final meeting, you will discuss possible next steps to continue your spiritual growth. Use this page to write any commitments you make to wear the armor in your everyday life.

ARMOR PIECE	To continue wearing this piece of armor, I will:
Belt of truth	
Breastplate of righteousness	
Feet sandaled with the gospel of peace	
Shield of faith	
Helmet of salvation	
Sword of the Spirit	
Praying for all	

THE ABCs OF SALVATION

Some people think a personal relationship with God is something only theologians can comprehend. Actually, God's plan of salvation is simple enough for everyone to understand. Here are the ABCs of salvation.

 ## Admit

Admit to God that you are a sinner. Each of us has a problem the Bible calls sin. Sin is a refusal to acknowledge God's authority over our lives. Everyone who does not live a life of perfect obedience to the Lord is guilty of sin. "All have sinned and fall short of the glory of God" (Rom. 3:23). Since none of us is perfect, all of us are sinners (Rom. 3:10-18). All persons need salvation.

The result of sin is spiritual death. "The wages of sin is death, but the gift of God is eternal life in Christ Jesus our Lord" (Rom. 6:23). Spiritual death means eternal separation from God. By God's perfect standard we are guilty of sin and therefore subject to the punishment for sin, which is separation from God. Admitting that you are a sinner and separated from God is the first step of repentance, which is turning from sin and self and turning toward God.

 ## Believe

Believe in Jesus Christ as God's Son and receive Jesus' gift of forgiveness from sin. In the death of Jesus on the cross, God provided salvation for all who would repent of their sins and believe in Jesus. "For God loved the world in this way: He gave His one and only Son, so that everyone who believes in Him will not perish but have eternal life" (John 3:16). God loves each of us. God offers us salvation. Although we have done nothing to deserve His love and salvation, God wants to save us.

 ## Confess

Confess your faith in Jesus Christ as Savior and Lord. After you have received Jesus Christ into your life, share your decision with another person. Tell your pastor or a Christian friend about your decision. Following Christ's example, ask for baptism by immersion in your local church as a public expression of your faith. "If you confess with your mouth, 'Jesus is Lord,' and believe in your heart that God raised Him from the dead, you will be saved. With the heart one believes, resulting in righteousness, and with the mouth one confesses, resulting in salvation" (Rom. 10:9-10).

If you have just prayed to receive Jesus Christ as your Savior and Lord, tell your pastor, small-group leader, or a Christian friend. This person will be able to guide your first steps as a new believer and pray for you. Remember: The Enemy doesn't like what you have done. Daily wear the full armor of God and ask for protection from temptation and the Enemy's lies. You are a new creation in Christ (2 Cor. 5:17).

Leader Guide

The leader guide for *Putting on the Armor: Equipped and Deployed for Spiritual Warfare* offers teaching suggestions for the group facilitator. Teaching plans include an introductory session and seven weekly group sessions to help process what participants have learned during individual study through the week. Leader guide suggestions are designed for 1 to 1½ hours of interaction, depending on the depth of discussion.

Nothing ensures the success of group discussion more than a covering of prayer and preparation. Being well-prepared includes submitting your planning and teaching to the Holy Spirit who already knows what participants need to make them equipped and deployed for spiritual warfare.

You can be assured that every believer in your group has experienced spiritual warfare—whether he or she knew what to call it. Your church may have been confronted with battles incited by Satan. As the Holy Spirit is allowed to direct your preparation and teaching, God's purposes for this study will be accomplished.

Goals for Group Discussion

- encouraging the full engagement and participation of every learner;
- personalizing the application of learning so lives are changed and spiritual growth occurs;
- equipping learners with a basic understanding of the nature of spiritual warfare and the armor God provides to every believer;
- challenging learners to employ God's armor as a natural extension of their daily Christian walk;
- inviting learners to deepen their understanding of the Book of Ephesians.

Course Format

Each week begins with a story about the Miller family. If you choose, you may debrief the story at the beginning or the end of each session—or you may not use it in the group. Each week contains five days of interactive study. Communicate to learners the necessity of completing each day's **individual learning activities**. The heart of the study focuses on Ephesians 6:10-20, but the author leads learners to understand the greater context of these verses in the Book of Ephesians.

Paul's letter to the church at Ephesus is crucial to understanding the power available to believers who experience spiritual warfare. Learners will be directed to an optional segment for "**More In-Depth Study.**"

These segments provide opportunities to develop greater insights into a theme or a specific passage in Ephesians. Encourage participants to study this portion as they see it from time to time.

Each day of study concludes with an optional "**Daily in the Word**" component. Studied consistently, this part of the learning experience will guide participants through a systematic study of the entire Book of Ephesians. At the end of each day members will find a memory verse taken from "Daily in the Word." If you use the memory verse cards on page 159, make a copy of page 160, "Christian Growth Study Plan," to give members at the last group session. Instructions for use of the CGSP are described at the top of page 160.

Additional learning aids such as definitions, main points, and Scriptures are available in the **side bars** of the study. Invite learners to consider this material as a useful source of information for them. Encourage learners to use their own Bibles in daily and group study.

Participation in **group discussion sessions** is a valuable asset to the learning experience. While the book can be completed by individuals, group discussions provide a platform for clarifying concepts, discovering practical application, and learning from one another. Encourage participants' regular attendance.

This study is essential for born-again believers. Since unbelievers are not protected by God's armor, the author has included the **plan of salvation** on page 147. Be prepared to present the "ABCs of Salvation" to any unbeliever who is in your group. Plan a time to privately visit with the individual or schedule a time with your pastor.

Members will be encouraged to consider finding **accountability partners** during this study. Be prepared to explain this concept and the benefits offered. See day 5 of week 1. They will also be asked to fill out a **prayer-request card** and exchange it with a different member each week. (See page 149, Concluding the Session, #2 for more details.) Bring blank cards to each session.

Introductory Session
Preparing for the Session
1. Pray for your group session.
2. Preview the content and learning activities in the member book.
3. Obtain and prepare required instructional materials:
   - Flip chart with tear sheets, marker board, or other surface
   - Index cards for prayer-request exchange

4. Provide one copy of *Putting on the Armor: Equipped and Deployed for Spiritual Warfare* for each person.
5. Provide reusable name tags (optional), an attendance sheet, extra Bibles, and writing materials.
6. Develop a process for collecting and recording payment for member books.
7. On your flip chart or other surface, write the definition and principles found in step 7 of "During the Session." Prepare to display it at the proper time.

During the Session

1. Direct participants to a table to sign the attendance sheet; take a name tag, Bible, and writing implement; and obtain their copy of the member book.
2. Welcome members and begin the session on time with prayer.
3. Write the phrase "WE ARE AT WAR!" on a tear sheet.
4. Ask, *"Is this a relevant statement in our culture today?"* Briefly discuss current manifestations of cultural, political, and spiritual conflict.
5. Ask, *"When engaged in a conflict, why do we need to: (a) accurately identify our enemy? (b) understand the reasons for the conflict? (c) determine strategies for victory?"*
6. Invite members to find Ephesians 6:10-20 in their Bibles. Explain that this passage is the heart of the study. Invite a volunteer to read the passage. Then ask, *"How do these verses (a) define spiritual warfare? (b) accurately identify our enemy? (c) recognize our primary strategy for victory?"*
7. Post the following operational definition of spiritual warfare and the basic principles to be clarified during the study. **Spiritual Warfare:** *The supernatural conflict caused by the opposition of Satan and his followers to the sovereignty of God, His will, and His people.* Discuss how this definition relates to Ephesians 6:10-13.
   Basic Principles of the Study
   - *Believers face schemes of a real enemy.*
   - *God has provided every spiritual weapon necessary for the believer's victory.*
   - *Empowerment for victory comes as we use the spiritual armor God provides to every believer.*
   - *Victory is gained when the believer correctly employs the spiritual weapons of God's armor.*
   - *Every believer, once equipped, is expected to be deployed in the battle against Satan.*
   Discuss or clarify these principles as needed.
8. Direct members to turn to the Table of Contents on page 3 of the member book. Explain that the study spends one week on each piece of the armor of God, so that members will know how to be equipped and deployed for victory in daily spiritual warfare.

9. Conduct a tour of the member book, emphasizing the following:
   - "Meet the Author," page 4
   - "Introduction," page 5
   - The daily format of the study (day 1–day 5)
   - "More In-Depth Study," page 9
   - "Daily in the Word," page 21
   - Memory Verse for This Week, page 21
   - Side-bar helps (for example, pp. 12,19)
   - "Reviewing the Full Armor of God" in side bars (see pp. 26,46)
10. Pair and Share. Have members turn to a partner of the same gender and share with one another their responses to these discussion prompts:
    - One issue I hope to study/understand
    - One idea I've already learned/gained from our discussion
    - One piece of armor that most intrigues me
    Invite one pair to summarize their discussion.

Concluding the Session

1. Reread Ephesians 6:18 aloud. Emphasize the importance of prayer in spiritual warfare and as a way of strengthening one's personal study time. Encourage the use of prayer during the week.
2. Distribute index cards and direct members to write a brief prayer request for their spiritual growth and sign it. Have them exchange cards with the promise to pray during the week over that request and write a note of encouragement or a Scripture verse on the back of the request cards. Members will return the card the following week. Even writing, "I prayed for you this week," will encourage accountability in praying for one another.
3. Lead a prayer for discerning the truths of the study.

Session 1—The Belt of Truth
Preparing for the Session

1. Pray for your group session.
2. Preview the content and learning activities in the member book.
3. For each session have on hand the index cards, attendance sheet, extra Bibles, and writing material.
4. Obtain and prepare required materials:
   - *Who Do You Say I Am?* Number 3x5 index cards with the following Scripture references. No card 1 is needed since the worksheet cites the references for statement 1. (Card 2: Isaiah 7:14; Matthew 1:18,20,24-25; Romans 1:3-4; Card 3: 2 Corinthians 5:21; Hebrews 4:15; 7:26; 1 Peter 2:22; Card 4: John 1:1-4; 10:30; Titus 2:13;

Hebrews 1:3; Card 5: Hebrews 2:17; 1 John 2:2; 4:10; Card 6: 1 Corinthians 15:3-8). See week 1, page 25 and activity 6 in "During the Session" for directions on how to use the cards.

- *Get Help!* Set up a display table using examples of various Bible helps, including the items from the list on page 13 of the member book or others you are able to obtain from your church library or your pastor. Consider displaying various Bibles that contain helps including study notes, concordances, or maps. If possible, have several Bible translations. LifeWay recommends the Holman Christian Standard Bible (HCSB), and your author has used this translation as the main text of the study. Have a sign at the table that says "GET HELP!" in large letters.

During the Session
1. Direct members to sign the attendance sheet and pick up their reusable name tag, Bible, or writing resources. (This instruction should be automatic after session 1.)
2. Welcome members and begin on time with prayer.
3. Recount the basic story line of the famous Danish fairy tale written by Hans Christian Anderson, *The Emperor's New Clothes*. The emperor is swindled by two tailors, who convince him and an entire village that if they cannot see his new clothes made from an exquisite invisible fabric, they are all foolish. Since no one wants to appear foolish, everyone pretends they can see his clothes as the emperor parades through town naked. Finally one innocent young boy declares, "He has nothing on!" and exposes the trickery of the tailors. Of course, all are faced with their true foolishness in falling for the ridiculous scheme. Relate this story to the topic of our study by discussing the following points:
   - The Enemy can trick us into believing we're wearing sufficient armor when really we're walking naked through the spiritual realm.
   - The Enemy attempts to "swindle" believers by getting them to trade the real armor of God for counterfeit coverings. Name some of these threadbare clothes. Examples include pride, defensiveness, self-sufficiency, biblical illiteracy, unbelief, ignorance regarding spiritual warfare or the Devil's schemes.
   - Review Ephesians 6:11-12 (margin, p. 6). Ask, *"From your study this week, why is it crucial to put on the full armor of God?"* (Only when wearing the whole armor of God are we properly and fully attired to engage in a very real battle with a very real enemy.)

4. Elaborate on the seven truths about the armor of God listed on page 10 of the member book.
5. Ask, *"How did day 2 help you understand the importance of studying and believing God's Word?"*
6. Ask, *"How would you have responded to Jordan's statement that Jesus was just a teacher?"* (top of p. 14).
7. Day 3 is the heart of week 1. Read Matthew 16:13-20 aloud. Repeat Christ's question in verse 15, *"'But what about you?' He asked, 'Who do you say I am?'"* The whole of Christianity ultimately rests on this question. Review the false statements about Christ listed on page 25 of the member book. Divide members into five pairs or small groups. Give each group a numbered index card with Scripture verse(s) that correspond to the numbered statements (see #2 in Preparing for the Session). Assign each pair or group one or more of the false statements to analyze. Direct groups to use their Bibles to look up their verses and work together to fill in the blanks assigned to them.
8. Allow time for groups to report their findings by (a) reading their assigned false statement, (b) describing Satan's scheme, (c) reading their verses, and (d) giving Christ's identity. Others should fill in the charts as each group reports. Suggest these Scriptures as prompts for struggling groups: Isa. 7:14; Matt, 1:8,20,24-25; John 1:1-4; Rom. 1:3-4; 10:30; 1 Cor. 15:3-8; 16:54-58; Titus 2:13; Heb. 1:3, 2:17; 4:15; 7:36; 1 Pet. 2:22; 1 John 4:10. Conclude this activity by asking Christ's question again, "What about you? Who do you say I am?" and reading the list of names under Christ's identity. Pause to pray at this point to thank Christ for who He is.
9. Read this statement from day 2, page 13: "Only when we understand and apply God's Word properly can we wear the belt of truth." As the group turns to James 1:22, ask, *"How does this statement relate to this verse?"* Notice that the verse in James states that unless we are obedient to God's Word, we are deceiving ourselves and don't have the truth!
10. Review the three ways Jesus is our model of righteousness (p. 19 in the member book). Discuss how each of those patterns in Jesus' life gives us hope and practical help for living in righteousness. Explain that the concept of living righteously will be explored more fully in week 2.

Concluding the Session
1. Review this week's memory verse. Say it together. Have members brainstorm specific spiritual blessings we have in Christ. Review "Steps for Memorizing The Word" in the side bar on page 19.

2. Encourage members to analyze each week's Scripture as they memorize it. Explain that understanding the verse will help them memorize it. If time allows, you may want to work through the steps as a group to provide an example.

3. If you are going to encourage accountability partners (as your author recommended), develop a plan for matching partners who want to participate. Use material from day 5 for clarification or procedures.

4. Take time to write and exchange prayer requests (index cards). Make sure members give the one they took last week to the original person.

5. Direct members' attention to the "GET HELP" display table. Briefly describe the materials you've provided. Allow enough time before the end of the session to let members browse through the items. Stay on hand to show how materials can be used.

6. Before dismissing the group to view the displayed materials, close in prayer.

Session 2—The Breastplate of Righteousness

Preparing for the Session
1. Pray.
2. Complete the activities in the member book and thoroughly study the suggested group discussion prompts and activities.
3. Photocopy the case studies found on page 152, one for every member of the group. Cut the columns in half. Store the second column for use in session 3.

During the Session
1. Welcome members and begin the session on time with prayer.
2. Read "Reviewing the Full Armor of God" in the margin on page 26. Ask, "*Can we know truth without knowing Jesus?*" (No. There is no truth apart from God's truth—He is truth!) "*What does it mean to live the Word?*" (obey it completely)
3. Direct members to the activity on page 27 where they described how Jesus lived. Invite members to share responses to that activity.
4. Allow volunteers to cite obstacles they circled and one example from the activity in the middle of page 29.
5. Instruct members to look at the last activity on page 29. Ask them to read silently their one sentence response in the margin of their books. Then under that sentence ask members to number 1, 2, 3 and rate themselves on a scale of 1 to 5 (1 = low, 5 = high) as you read aloud these questions. (1) *How well are you obeying Him in this matter?* Allow time to mark answers. (2) *To what degree*

do you desire to be obedient in this matter? Allow time to mark answers. (3) *To what degree do you believe you are able to be obedient in this matter?* Conclude by reading aloud the sentence in the margin on page 29.

Optional: If you are using accountability partners, encourage them to discuss the above activity.

6. Case Studies: Ask members to form three small groups. Assign one of the case studies to each group. Instruct members to read their assigned story and follow the directions. After appropriate discussion time, allow the group reporter to briefly explain their analyses to the whole group. Since everyone has a copy, members of other groups may want to insert a comment or suggestion.

7. Determine if the case studies followed the pattern of Joseph's thinking described on page 36 of the member book. Invite the groups to develop a similar chart for their selected case study.

8. Review the activity at the top of page 38. Use a voting process to see which excuse the group thinks is most common. Elaborate on the choice with the most votes, discussing why that excuse is so prevalent. Discuss what corrective thinking/action is necessary to avoid that temptation.

9. Review the cycle of sin evident in David's life. Ask, "*What was the first chink in his armor? What was the good news for David? How is that news even better for us as New Testament believers?*"

Concluding the Session
1. Ask for any additional insight from members who completed the "Daily in the Word" segment this week.
2. Review this week's memory verse. Ask, "*How would a spirit of wisdom and revelation help us keep the breastplate of righteousness firmly fastened? Are there any other insights from meditating on the memory verse?*"
3. Ask for volunteers to quote the memory verses from weeks 1 and 2.
4. Exchange prayer-requests cards.
5. Close with prayer.

Session 2: Case Studies about Temptation

Read the case study assigned to your group. As you discuss your case, identify the following: (a) the primary temptation described in the situation, (b) Satan's targeted strategy (see pp. 31-33 for the three strategies studied this week), (c) What your group thinks will probably happen to the characters.

1. Rod and Julie purchased a new home and began some remodeling projects. They can do much of the work themselves and love to demonstrate their creativity, making them a great team. Since both work outside the home, weekends provide the perfect blend of together time and the unbroken blocks of time needed for the bigger projects. Their Sunday School class has consistently called and sent notes encouraging the couple to come back, and Rod and Julie appreciate their thoughtfulness. They know their absence won't last forever. They just need the rest of the summer and fall to focus on the house; then they'll jump right back into all the church activities they used to love.

2. Kathy, a Christian, is 32 and single. She was beginning to wonder if she would ever marry and have children until Todd appeared on the scene. She was immediately drawn to his sense of humor and fun-loving nature. They started dating, casually at first, but Kathy definitely anticipates they will soon be discussing marriage. As she gets ready for every date, she has begun to experience increasing unrest. She has a verbal battle with herself. "Kathy, you know he's not a Christian," she tells herself. "I know, but maybe he'll get saved. He's talked about going to my church soon." She's thought of dozens of reasons to keep the relationship alive, but one nagging argument keeps returning—Todd is not a believer.

3. Steve is a long-time active member of the church and a businessman in town. He is well-respected among his peers for his assets in the business world—having high motivation and being competitive by nature. On the surface, you would think Steve couldn't be in any better stage of life. Sadly, on the inside Steve is miserable. Knowing how important image is, Steve concentrates on looking sharp and being sharp. He puts a positive spin on his week's sales, embellishing just a bit. Office parties at his colleagues' homes are terrible reminders that his house is meager compared to theirs. He always tries to park his SUV next to Charlie's sedan rather than Brady's new convertible. No matter how hard he tries, Steve always feels like a failure. He's just hoping no one will notice.

Session 3: My Witnessing Profile

Using a scale of 1-5, with 5 being the highest, indicate how strongly you agree with the following statements.

____ 1. I believe that people without Christ will be eternally separated from God.

____ 2. I feel a personal responsibility to witness to those who don't know Christ as Savior.

____ 3. I am comfortable talking to nonbelievers about Christ.

____ 4. I feel prepared to share the gospel with a lost person.

____ 5. I know Scriptures that present the plan of salvation (like the Roman Road).

____ 6. I have an interest in taking training courses or workshops in evangelism through my church.

____ 7. I have witnessed to a lost person during the last year.

____ 8. People respond positively when I share the gospel with them.

____ 9. My lifestyle matches my testimony about Christ and Christian living.

____ 10. I've begun an activity (like taking up a hobby or joined a civic group) to develop relationships with unbelievers.

____ 11. My biggest strength in my witnessing profile is courage.

____ 12. I regularly pray for unbelievers I know.

_____ Add your total.

If you score below 12 points, choose 1 or 2 areas to work on during this study. If you have an accountability partner, share your responses with him or her.

If you score between 12 and 24 points, select your lowest score and set some goals for improvement in that area during this study.

If you score between 25 and 60, ask God to show you how to mentor another believer in witnessing skills. While you share your testimony, the other person will silently pray for you and the person hearing the good news about Jesus Christ.

Session 3—Feet Sandaled with the Gospel of Peace

Preparing for the Session

1. Pray.
2. Complete the activities in the member book and then thoroughly study the suggested group discussion prompts and activities.
3. Obtain and prepare the materials required for the following activities:
   - An odds-and-ends collection of shoes—different sizes, men's, women's, and children's (4-6 total).
   - Poster or board on which to draw the chart described in #8 in "During the Session." You will need to make three placards (standard paper size) using construction paper or card stock. Print the statements numbered (1), (2), and (3), omitting the answers. Have tape available to affix placards to poster or board. The spaces with question marks in the diagram are there to show the placement of the three placards.
4. Photocopy "My Witnessing Profile" on page 152 if you did not do so in preparation for session 2. Distribute one to each class member.
5. Enlist a volunteer to share his or her testimony based on the outline provided on pages 62-63.

During the Session

1. Welcome members and begin the session on time with prayer.
2. Restate "Reviewing the Full Armor of God" in the margin on page 46. Ask, *"What relationship exists between the belt of truth and the breastplate of righteousness? Can one be worn effectively without the other?"* Elaborate if responses aren't forthcoming.
3. Display the assortment of shoes prepared in advance. Ask a volunteer to come to the display. Ask the volunteer to pick out one of the shoes that might fit. (No need to try it on!) Then pick up a shoe that is obviously too big or too little and ask, "How about this one?" Try to convince the volunteer to choose a shoe that would not fit or is for the opposite sex. Suggest the desirability of the other shoes. Then say, *"If all the shoes would fit you, which would you choose and why?"* The volunteer will probably pick a shoe based on either appearance or practicality. Thank the volunteer and let him or her be seated.
4. Ask the group, *"How important is it to have shoes that fit well, look good, and serve a purpose?"* The group will affirm that all features are important at times. Explain that God wants us to have the right spiritual shoes to be perfectly fitted for our task!
5. Ask, *"How does being properly 'sandaled' prepare us for the spiritual realities of our world?"* Discuss some of the members' responses to the activity on page 48 and the author's points on that page.
6. Ask, *"What's the spiritual difference between standing on the defensive and moving out on the offensive?"*
7. Ask, *"How are we at war with God if we are apart from Christ as Savior? How does a correct understanding help us explain salvation to a person who (a) believes in God, but not in Christ as Savior? (b) believes being good is enough to get into heaven?"*
8. Display the poster and the three placards (described in #3 "Preparing for the Session"). You may choose to form three groups or let everyone express an opinion in game-style competition.

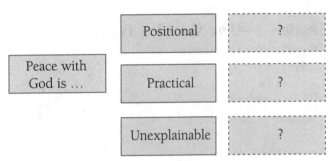

Randomly assign passages to be read (given as answers below). Then let members or groups match the placards to each space with a question mark. The result will be a correct description of peace:
   (1) In Christ I become God's child.
      (Answer: positional. Eph. 1:11,14)
   (2) In Christ I am created for good works/holiness
      (Answer: practical. Eph. 2:10; Heb. 10:24)
   (3) In Christ I have peace in all circumstances.
      (Answer: unexplainable. 2 Thess. 3:16; Phil. 4:7)

   Invite one or two group members to share about a time when they experienced unexplainable peace.
9. Ask, *"How does our peace with God spill over into other relationships?"* (Use passages in margin, p. 54.)
10. Pair and Share. Read the steps to forgiving others on page 56. Ask members to turn to a partner of the same sex and share responses to the activity at the top of page 57.
11. Ask, *"How does Satan try to disarm us when we try to witness to the lost?"* List members' responses on a tear sheet. (List may include fear of rejection, lies about the lost condition of all people, our own guilt, diffuses our boldness in witnessing, and distracts us.) Ask, *"What impact would praying the acrostic GOD'S HEART (p. 60) have on Satan's disarming tactics?"*

11. Call on the person you enlisted in advance to give a testimony.
12. Hand out copies of "My Witnessing Profile." Ask members to fill out the sheet individually. Without discussing their answers, ask them what they might do to change some of these answers to a "5."

Concluding the Session
1. Ask for any additional insight from members who completed the "Daily in the Word" segment.
2. Review this week's memory verse. Ask, *"How could you restate this in your own words? Can you share any other insights from meditating on the memory verse?"*
3. Exchange prayer-request cards.
4. Close with prayer.

Session 4—The Shield of Faith
Preparing for the Session
1. Pray.
2. Complete the activities in the member book and thoroughly study the suggested group discussion prompts and activities.

During the Session
1. Welcome members and begin the session on time with prayer.
2. Connect the opening scenario on page 66 with the pieces of armor listed in the margin. Ask for members' responses to the questions posed at the end of the scenario. Ask, *"What pieces of God's armor will be most helpful to the Millers as they make their decision?"*
3. Ask a volunteer to read Ephesians 6:16 (margin, p. 67). Ask, *"What one word in that verse indicates the strength of the shield of faith?"* (All) Discuss the implications of this fact—that faith extinguishes *all* the "flaming arrows of the evil one."
4. Review the definition of faith provided by the author on page 67. Pair and Share: Direct members to turn to a partner (not a spouse) and share examples of how faith became a reality in their lives. The bulleted points from pages 67-68 can help shape their discussion. Give two to four minutes for sharing, then conclude the Pair and Share time.
5. Read the paragraph after the bulleted list (top of p. 68). Ask, *"What makes this kind of faith so powerful against the Enemy?"* (This kind of faith rests on who God is and what He can do—not on ourselves or our circumstances. It accesses the power of God.)
6. Discuss members' responses to the questions at the top of page 69. From day 2 (p. 71), ask volunteers to share where they rated their church on a fortress

mentality. Discuss ways your church can break down any areas where a fortress mentality exists.
7. Summarize: We are not to cloister ourselves inside the walls of the church building. Rather we are to march out confidently believing that not even the gates of hell (death and Satan's ultimate weapon) will hinder the growth of the Church.
8. Review the section "Faith is an Action Word" (pp. 71-72) and the section of day 3 describing Abraham's faith (p. 75). Ask, *"What price did some of these biblical characters pay to exercise their faith? Do you know someone now who is paying a price for their faith? What rewards will be theirs?"*
9. Direct members to turn to page 29 of their books. Ask them to reflect on what they wrote in the margin. (See session 2, activity 5.) Instruct them to return to page 75 and ask, *"Do any of these faith challenges need to be addressed, too? Do you need God to increase your faith to respond with a specific action?"* Invite members to consider sharing their need on their prayer-request cards later in the session so someone can be praying specifically for the faith to be obedient.
10. Ask, *"How is worry a lack of faith in God? How can we learn to lay our worries down?"* (By picking up the shield of faith!) Discuss the incompatibility of worry and faith. Direct members to the worksheet "Deflecting Worry" on page 85. Discuss the various attributes of God the members listed. Have them explain how these traits increase our faith in God to take care of our worries. Emphasize that the graphics of this worksheet remind us that worry is one of the flaming arrows from the Enemy. Our shield is in God's character—who He is and what He can do. When we are tempted to worry, our defense is to concentrate on God's nature.
11. Refer to the author's question on page 81, asking members to reflect on what they have learned during this study. Give members three minutes to quickly scan their books looking for notes, underlining, or starred items. Ask them to record in the margin of page 81 three of the most significant insights they've gained. Divide members into pairs or groups of three and have them share their insights with each other.

Concluding the Session
1. Ask for any additional insight from members who completed the "Daily in the Word" segment.
2. Review this week's memory verse. Invite volunteers to say the verse from memory. Have the whole group repeat the verse together. Ask, *"What relationship exists between 'walking worthy of our calling' and*

exercising faith every day? Any other insights from meditating on the memory verse?"

3. Exchange prayer-request cards.
4. Close with prayer.

Session 5—The Helmet of Salvation

Preparing for the Session

1. Pray
2. Complete the activities in the member book and thoroughly study the suggested group discussion prompts and activities.
3. Obtain and prepare required materials for the following activities:
   - Prepare five review placards or poster strips to display on a wall or board. Write the title of one day's study on each placard (see #2 in "During the Session").
   - Be prepared to display and discuss the worksheet titled "The Sifting Process" described in #6 below (see p. 100). Draw a large circle in the center of the tear sheet. Place eight dots evenly spaced on the line of the circle beginning at the top of the circle. Starting at the top dot write *living in faith*. Moving clockwise around the circle write one of the following statements by each dot. (2) *Enemy attacks—our guard is down*; (3) *faith falters*; (4) *sin, denying Christ in word or deed*; (5) *God intervenes*; (6) *heartfelt repentance*; (7) *God forgives and restores*; (8) *joy in our walk of salvation*. Between each statement draw an arrow shape on the line of the circle showing the clockwise direction of the sifting process.

During the Session

1. Welcome members and begin the session on time with prayer.
2. Direct members' attention to the display of review placards. Use them to initiate discussion of the key point of each day's study. The review of these key points may open the way for an unsaved member's conversion. Be sensitive to the depth of discussion needed for your group as you review: (1) Understanding Who We Were (our sinful condition before we accepted Christ), (2) Understanding What God Did (God initiates salvation), (3) Understanding Who We Are in Christ (our very nature changes as a result of our salvation), (4) Wearing the Helmet Daily (salvation is a one-time spiritual rebirth experience, but we are called to walk in the joy, assurance, and victory of our salvation every day), (5) Living in Hope (understanding the difference between momentary discouragement and spiritual defeat). During discussion emphasize the critical nature of this

piece of armor. To live victoriously now and eternally, this piece of armor must be secure.

3. Ask, *"Why do we need to remember our condition before we were saved?"* (See top paragraphs, p. 87.) Lead the group to brainstorm specific results of the three primary descriptors of our lost condition (examples in parentheses).
   - Blindness—(we were unable to see God's hand in our lives, we didn't understand who Christ was or what He really did, we didn't see any relationship between our circumstances and God's sovereignty)
   - Living in Satan's Dark Domain—(we made choices that were contrary to God's will for our lives, we didn't serve God, we didn't love God, we didn't enjoy being with Christians, we didn't read or understand God's Word as a guide for living and relating to God, we didn't experience fellowship with God or the Holy Spirit)
   - Living in Bondage to Satan's Influence—(we believed the lies of the Enemy; we lived corrupt or sinful lifestyles; we used unwholesome language; we were inclined toward sin rather than holiness; we tolerated, accommodated, or encouraged others' ungodly lifestyles)
4. From day 2 ask for responses to the learning activity on page 93. Summarize God's plan for us and our response when we wear the helmet of salvation. Review the activity and side bar on page 94.
   - Task: Small groups will brainstorm false messages Christians are tempted to believe that distort who we are in Christ. Members will organize these false messages under three headings that indicate the truth of who we are in Christ: *Loved, Forgiven,* and *Changed.*
   - Method: On a tear sheet write the three headings you want the groups to copy. Before grouping, briefly discuss what these headings mean—unconditional love from God, being completely forgiven of all sin, and being forever changed through the power of the indwelling Holy Spirit. (See day 3 for help.) Provide the whole group an example of a false message under each heading:
     - Loved—I'm too bad a person for God to really love me;
     - Forgiven—there are some sins God will not forgive;
     - Changed—I cannot break some of the bad habits I've formed.

   Instruct groups to choose someone who will record for them. Divide members into group of four to five people. Distribute one sheet of blank paper to each group and have the recorders write titles for three headings at the top of the sheet. Provide adequate time for group discussion. At the end of the activity, you may want to invite each group to share one false message under each of the three headings.

5. Remaining in small groups, direct members to page 99 of their member books. Review the three steps to following Jesus written in the margin. Assign one of the steps to each small group. Allow time for them to list as many practical ways believers can take those steps in their daily lives. (Recorder can list responses on the back of the sheet used in the previous activity.) Have a member of each group report two or three of their group's best ideas after allowing four to five minutes for this activity. If needed, groups can refer to pages 98-99 for help.

6. Review the process of sifting as described in day 4. Display the tear sheet titled "The Sifting Process" that you prepared in advance. Instruct members to replicate the diagram on the tear sheet in the margin on page 100 of their books. Briefly explain each step in the process or ask a volunteer to explain what happens in each step. After members have discussed and copied each step of this process ask the following questions, leaving time for responses after each one. *"What can we do to keep our guard up without being overly confident as Peter was? What would be an appropriate action when our faith begins to falter that would short-circuit sin? What are some of the ways God intervenes in a Christian's life to bring the believer to heart-felt repentance? Why do some believers fail to consistently demonstrate joy in their salvation? Why does God allow this sifting process?"*

7. Direct members to day 5, which discusses how discouragement happens even to believers. Remind members that when our guard is down, the Enemy uses discouragement to erode our hope and our joy. Ask, *"How does the helmet of salvation ward off discouragement?"* If time permits conduct a brief study of Hebrews 11:32–12:2. This passage gives the reader an astonishing picture of God's faithful followers. Focus on Hebrews 12:1-2. Ask the following questions. *"Who are the witnesses described as a large cloud? How do these witnesses spur us to faith and hope? How is Jesus described in this passage? Based on this passage what helped Christ endure the cross on our behalf? How does this passage encourage you?"*

8. Direct members to the "More In-Depth Study" activity on page 89 in the member book. This activity is an extension to activity #4 but focuses on the unbeliever rather than a believer who succumbs to false messages from the Enemy. This activity will strengthen members'

attempts to witness to people who expression common objections to the Gospel message. If time is limited, you may want to replace activity #7 with this one.

Concluding the Session

1. Ask for any additional insight from members who completed the "Daily in the Word" segment this week.
2. Review this week's memory verse. Have the whole group repeat the verse together. Ask, *"If we forgave others as Christ forgave us, how would our relationships with other be different? Any other insights from meditating on the memory verse?"*
3. The content of this week's session may encourage unbelievers in your group to accept Christ as Savior. Offer the invitation to visit with anyone who wants to discuss salvation privately with you or with the pastor. Let the group know that if someone wants more information they can see you after the class or call to arrange a meeting.
4. Exchange prayer-requests cards.
5. Close with prayer.

Session 6—The Sword of the Spirit
Preparing for the Session
1. Pray.
2. Complete the activities in the member book and thoroughly study the suggested group discussion prompts and activities.
3. If you choose to use the five case studies in #9, make enough copies for each group member.

During the Session
1. Welcome members and begin on time with prayer.
2. Pair and Share. Instruct members to pair with someone of the same sex and pick one bulleted point from "Reviewing the Full Armor of God" on page 106. Ask each pair to share one plan for improvement.
3. Day 1 lists three ways God's Word teaches us. As a group, discuss how each method of instruction is valuable to the believer. Here are some prompts.
   - who God is. (See the list of God's attributes on pp. 107-108.) Ask, *"How will an understanding of these attributes help us when we don't understand what is happening in our lives?"*
   - God is sovereign over the Enemy. Instruct members to find the verses referenced under this subtopic in their Bibles. Select one or more members to read them to the group. Summarize: *"God has a greater purpose when He allows the Enemy to attack (Rom. 8:29). Even the Enemy's attacks are subject to God's will (Gen. 50:19-20). Battles with the Enemy are*

won in God's strength and not our own (2 Sam. 22:33)." Lead members to identify current life situations where these truths apply.

- God is greater (more powerful) than the Enemy. The Enemy's activities are always controlled and limited by God. Ask, *"How could you help someone whose circumstances are blinding them to this truth?"*

4. Identify the three strategies from day 2 that the Enemy uses to keep us from wielding God's Word in warfare. For each strategy listed, explain how memorizing Scripture would directly counter (and exceed) the Enemy's strategy. Ask, *"What is the natural result of not knowing Scripture?"*

5. Invite members to turn in their books to day 3. Ask, *"What is the difference among a reading, study, and learning plan? How are they different in terms of reading the Bible? Which insight will change something about the way you study God's Word?"* If available, bring copies of the recommended resources listed on page 114. Develop a way to share with the group other opportunities for Bible study your church offers. Consider displaying church brochures or having a staff member share small-group opportunities.

6. Ask the following questions, allowing time for answers after each one. *"Given the opening scenario in day 4, how would you have counseled Patrick if he had shared with you his feelings of defeat and discouragement? What specifics ways does our church encourage and restore those who falter?"*

7. Discuss the answers to the learning activities on pages 122 (concerning Zechariah) and 123.

8. Direct members to turn to the case study at the end of week 6. In pairs or groups of three, have them discuss the scenario, then determine what a believer would have to know about God's Word, the history of the church's past discipleship plan, and what is effectively addressing the situation now. When the groups are finished, invite them to report their findings.

9. If time permits assign the following case studies to one or more persons. Distribute copies to each member. The person named in each scenario is a believer. Debrief by having one person from each case study report what they would do in the situation. After groups have reported, ask, *"In your case study, did you struggle at all with knowing what the Bible teaches about the issues involved?"* Emphasize that we have to know and apply the Bible when we seek to help others.

A. Max has been invited to join some colleagues in a legal but ethically questionable business deal. The program could be very lucrative. None of the other colleagues involved are Christians.

B. June keeps a Bible on her desk to read during her lunch hour. It's provided several opportunities to witness to unbelievers. June's supervisor has become very critical of her lately. June believes the supervisor is resisting the open expression of June's faith.

C. Jason's friend has confided to him that he is thinking of having an affair with a woman he knows from the office. His friend attends a local church and professes to be a Christian. He has shared with Jason that he is in a joyless marriage.

D. John has been the pastor of his church for six years. He's felt led to preach a series of sermons that addressed areas where church members needed growth. Recently, he learned that a couple left the church because of his "volatile" sermons.

E. Linda received a call from a friend who was not living a godly lifestyle. Her friend felt she was under spiritual attack and was feeling miserable. She asked Linda if they could have lunch together to talk.

Concluding the Session
1. Ask for additional insight from members who completed the "Daily in the Word" segment this week.
2. Review this week's memory verse. Ask, *"How does knowing God's Word help us walk as 'children of light?'"*
3. Exchange prayer-requests cards.
4. Close with prayer.

Session 7—The Power of Prayer
Preparing for the Session
1. Have copies of page 160 for each member.
2. Complete the activities in the member book and thoroughly study the suggested group discussion prompts and activities. Pray for the group members.
3. Obtain and prepare required materials for the following activities:
- Prepare placards and strips for Suit Up! described in #2. First, write the name of one piece of armor on each of six placards to affix to a board or wall. Display these placards far enough apart that several people can stand in front of each placard. Second, print or type the bulleted points under "Reviewing the Full Armor of God." Cut these apart with one bulleted point per strip. Mix up the strips. Put three or four strips in each of six envelopes. (See pages 126-27 for content.)

- You will need appropriate adhesive to affix the placards and the strips of paper. (Make sure your adhesive doesn't damage the wall!)
- Print or type the four reasons Paul urges his readers to pray as described in "During the Session" #4. Leave one blank in each statement.

During the Session

1. Welcome members and begin session with prayer.
2. Announce a group activity called "Suit Up!" Place members into six individual or small teams and give each an envelope. Without using the member book, challenge groups to place their bulleted points under the placard for the correct piece of the armor. This will provide a way for groups to review the points. Once all strips are placed on the wall or board, invite members to check their work (see pp. 126-27). Have them reorganize any misplaced strips.
3. Invite members to turn to the worksheet "Linking the Armor" on page 144. Reorganize members into pairs or groups of three. Assign each grouping two pieces of the armor of God. Challenge them to identify how their two pieces of armor relate to one another. Instruct them to follow the directions. While they work, write the following questions on a tear sheet or board for them to address during their discussion: (a) Is one piece of armor required to be in place before the other, or are they interdependent? (b) How does each piece of armor strengthen the other pieces? (c) Which piece of armor requires more discipline to wield effectively in warfare? (15 links or connections)
4. Review why Paul urged his readers to pray. Select four members to read and fill in the blanks of the sentences prepared in advance. Ask members to fill in the blanks and discuss the significance of each reason.
   - All believers battle against the <u>Enemy</u>. Discuss why all believers will face spiritual conflicts.
   - The battle will be <u>intense</u> (other words could be used). Ask, *"Why is prayer such a powerful weapon during intense battles?"*
   - Pray to praise God, <u>rejoicing</u> even in the middle of the battle. Ask, *"How does rejoicing strengthen our spiritual position in battle?"*
   - Paul understood the <u>brevity</u> of life. Ask, *"How does the familiar saying, 'Life is fragile. Handle with prayer.' relate to this statement?"*
5. Refer to page 129 in the member book. Ask, *"Why did the author encourage us to be alert before an Enemy attack? What can prayer accomplish when used prior to rather than following an attack?"*

6. Ask, *"Based on your study in day 2, what is your understanding of praying 'in the Spirit'? Is it possible to pray without the Spirit?"*
7. Review the ways on pages 134-35 to get a plan for prayer support. Display the prayer resources listed on page 135 if they are available to you. Brainstorm additional resources and ways to encourage strategic prayer for other believers.
8. Evaluate the effect of using the weekly prayer-request cards. Ask, *"How has this practice benefited you, either as a pray-er or as the recipient of prayers?"* Allow a brief time for testimonies of answered prayer.
9. Direct members to the "Know-Be-Do" worksheet on page 145. You may want to assign each piece of armor to small groups to complete and report, or analyze the worksheet as a whole group. Instruct groups to determine what the believer must KNOW about that piece of armor, what he must BE in order to effectively wear the piece, and what specific actions to DO while wearing it. Ask groups to relate the memory verse to their piece of armor.
10. Together complete the "Next Steps" on page 146.

Concluding the Session

1. Ask for any additional insight from members who completed the "Daily in the Word" segment.
2. Encourage the group to continue using accountability partners and prayer partners, and continue to be a prayer warrior for your church's staff and ministries.
3. Consider closing with an opportunity for those who want to may pray, or you may want to close the session by praying for each of the group members. Celebrate what they have contributed to this study.
4. Distribute copies of page 160 and give instructions for mailing them to LifeWay Christian Resources for Bible study credit.